Trivial Pursuit ™

The Movies

THE AUTHORIZED GAME BOOK

GUINNESS BOOKS ⟩⟩⟩

Design: Clive Sutherland
Design concept and cover design: Craig Dodd

© Guinness Superlatives Ltd and Horn Abbot International Limited 1987
Published in Great Britain by Guinness Superlatives Ltd,
33 London Road, Enfield, Middlesex

Printed in Great Britain by The Bath Press Ltd, Avon

'Guinness' is a registered trade mark of Guinness Superlatives Ltd

Trivial Pursuit is a game and trademark owned and licensed by Horn
Abbot International Limited

British Library Cataloguing in Publication Data
Trivial Pursuit : pocket edition : movies.
  1. Moving-pictures — Miscellanea
  791.43'076   PN1994

ISBN 0-85112-880-7

HORN ABBOT
INTERNATIONAL

Trivial Pursuit ™

New from Guinness — **The Pocket Edition of Trivial Pursuit!** The slimline Pocket Edition has been specially designed so that trivia fans can carry with them more than 1000 tantalizing trivia questions wherever they go. Now you can play Trivial Pursuit in the car, waiting for a bus, on a train, even in the bath — you need never be bored again.

Each Pocket Edition is arranged in quizzes, with the answers at the back of the book for easy reference. And to make sure that there's something for everyone there are three other separate titles — **Genus, Rock and Pop** and **Sport,** each containing hours of classic trivia challenge!

THE MOVIES EDITION

The Movies Pocket Edition contains 54 quizzes divided into six categories. The categories are coded:

(TT)	Themes and Titles
(MW)	Movie World
(SR)	Stars and Roles
(LT)	Lives and Times
(SS)	Silver Screen
(MM)	Making Movies

(1) What is the name of Tarzan's companion?

(2) What was the sequel to *Born Free*?

(3) Which movie was publicized with the slogan, 'The birds is coming!'?

(4) How did the shark die in *Jaws II*?

(5) What actually was the Pink Panther?

(6) What kind of animal was the star of *Ring of Bright Water*?

7 What kind of animal was Benji?

8 What animal is missing from the title of this Marx Brothers' movie — ..... *Feathers*?

9 Which well-armed creature appears in the title of a 'dear' Margaret Lockwood movie?

10 In which of her movies was Jane Fonda nearly pecked to death by birds?

11 What kind of animal was Tarka?

12 In which pirate role did Wallace Beery, Robert Newton and Orson Welles get the bird?

13 Which 'wabbit' started out as a hare?

14 What were Michael Caine and Olivia De Havilland attacked by in a disastrous 1978 disaster movie?

15 Which mystical movie was about a bird who flies fast, dies and achieves grace?

16 Which bird called Sylvester a 'puddy tat'?

17 What kind of animal co-starred in *Hannibal Brooks*?

18 On which famous horror writer's story was the 1941 movie *The Black Cat* based?

19 What was the name of Gene Autry's equine companion?

20 Which Tennessee Williams drama was turned into a movie starring Paul Newman and Elizabeth Taylor?

1 Which river did *A Bridge Too Far* span?

2 Which French port was the setting for *French Connection II*?

3 In which city did *The Sting* take place?

4 In which city is *Cabaret* set?

5 In which US state was *Gone with the Wind* set?

6 Which country provided the setting for the John Wayne movie *The Quiet Man*?

7 The star of *Death Wish* set out to clean up which city?

8 Which movie, starring Dustin Hoffman, was set in a Cornish village?

9 In which country was the final scene of *Butch Cassidy and the Sundance Kid* set?

10 Which city formed the world of Suzie Wong?

11 Which 1972 movie, starring Burt Reynolds, was shot on location on the Chattooga River in the Appalachians?

12 Which city was the setting for the Olympics in the movie *Chariots of Fire*?

13 In which city was *Ninotchka* set?

14 Which Long Island resort provides the setting for *Jaws*?

15 In which city is *Les Enfants du Paradis* set?

16 Which 1986 movie starring Robert de Niro was set in Paraguay?

17 In which US state is *Giant* set?

18 Which 1945 weepie, starring Celia Johnson and Trevor Howard, was set largely on a railway station?

19 In which valley was this film set?

20 Over which Italian city does *A Room With a View* look out?

1 Who starred as the heroic Reverend Frank Scott in *The Poseidon Adventure*?

2 Which star received top billing in *Gone with the Wind*?

3 In which disaster movie did Paul Newman and Steve McQueen star?

4 Who was the male star of *Top Gun*?

5 In which movie did these two sex symbols star together?

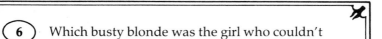

6 Which busty blonde was the girl who couldn't help it in *The Girl Can't Help It*?

7 Who starred as Hannah in Woody Allen's *Hannah and Her Sisters*?

8 Who received top billing in *The Graduate*?

9 Which British-born actor received top billing in the star-studded *Around the World in Eighty Days*?

10 Who starred as Mozart in *Amadeus*?

11 Which star came to dinner in *Guess Who's Coming to Dinner*?

12 Which British-born Hollywood star topped the credits in *Mona Lisa*?

13 Which actor starred as Tarzan in *Greystoke: The Legend of Tarzan, Lord of the Apes*?

14 Who starred in *A Man for All Seasons* and *Jaws*?

15 Who starred as Celie in *The Color Purple*?

16 Which actress starred in the ill-fated *Revolution*?

17 Who was propelled to fame in the title role of 1935's *Captain Blood*?

18 Who starred opposite Leonard Whiting in Franco Zefferelli's *Romeo and Juliet*?

19 Who played Sonny Corleone in *The Godfather*?

20 Who was the male star of *9½ Weeks*?

1 What should the movie *Krakatoa East of Java* have been more accurately called?

2 Which major MGM star had a 1930 contract specifying what time she should be in bed?

3 Which all time great movie was already being shot by the time its leading lady was cast?

4 Who donated the money to pay for a statue of Al Jolson in Los Angeles?

5 What have John Wayne, Burt Reynolds and Carol Channing all worn on screen?

6 Which star of *My Fair Lady* has a glass eye?

7 Which star turned down the role Dustin Hoffman grabbed in *The Graduate*?

8 Which star received 135 000 gifts on her eighth birthday?

9 At which screen star's 'lying in state' was the coffin surrounded by men in black shirts giving the Fascist salute?

10 What was actress Lucille Le Sueur rechristened after MGM ran a competition to find a name for her?

11 Which multi-millionaire spent $12 million trying to buy up all the copies of his epic Mogul flop *The Conqueror*, which had cost only $6 million to make?

12 Which western musical contains a scene for which scientists grew corn 16ft high?

13 For which 1986 Robert Redford movie were paintings worth $10 million used to dress the set?

(14) What was so special about the cast of the 1938 movie *The Terror of Tiny Town*?

(15) For which box-office flop did Michael Cimino shoot 220 hours of film at a cost of $57 million?

(16) In which 1974 movie did the real-life Baron Franckenstein appear under his screen name of Clement St George?

(17) Why didn't this Hollywood star collect his three Oscars for *Annie Hall* in person?

(18) Who had his ideas turned down by Louis B. Mayer because he thought that pregnant women would be frightened by a 10-foot tall rodent on screen?

(19) How many women were there in the 1961 movie *Seven Women from Hell*?

(20) Which star of *One Million Years BC* played a cavewoman in an uplift bra?

1. Which planet's moon was the destination in *2001: A Space Odyssey*?

2. Which 1970's sci-fi shocker was promoted with the line, 'In space no one can hear you scream'?

3. What age was terminal in the film *Logan's Run*?

4. Which futuristic film featured gangs of delinquents called Droogs?

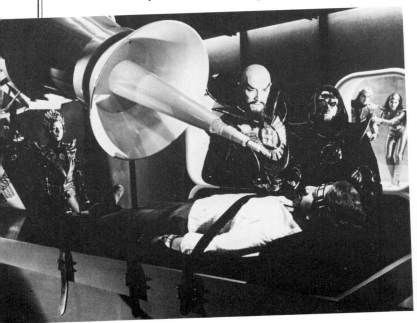

5. What is the name of this 25th-century villain, and which hero fights him?

6. What make of car was turned into a time machine in *Back to the Future*?

7. Which planet do Bud and Lou visit in *Abbott and Costello Go To Mars*?

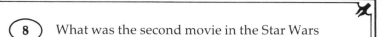

8 What was the second movie in the Star Wars trilogy?

9 Who played *The Man Who Fell to Earth*?

10 What was the sequel to *2001: A Space Odyssey*?

11 From which planet does Superman come?

12 Which actor's chest did the 'thing' burst out of in *Alien*?

13 Which zany sci-fi movie brought Woody Allen back to life after 2000 years?

14 Which of Jane Fonda's films was set in the 40th century?

15 Who played the futuristic L.A. cop in the 1982 film *Blade Runner*?

16 What was the title of Stanley Kubrick's 1968 movie, which took three and a half years to make?

17 What colour were the aliens' eyes in *Close Encounters of the Third Kind*?

18 Which Star Trek character was being sought in the film *Star Trek III* — a) Scotty   b) Mr Spock or c) Captain Kirk?

19 Which classic 1956 sci-fi film featured emotionless people who emerged from pods?

20 For which planet was *Battlestar Galactica* heading?

1 Which actress made her debut in *An Unseen Enemy* in 1912 and was still going strong in *Sweet Liberty* in 1986?

2 Who was the popular 'mixed-up' hero of early silent westerns?

3 Which 1936 movie satirized the horrors of the mechanical age?

4 Which country led the world in feature film production until 1911 — a) Australia b) Hungary or c) Great Britain?

5 Mary Pickford and Douglas Fairbanks were voted the most popular male and female stars in Russia — true or false?

6 Which silent police force was led by Ford Sterling?

7 Who was known as 'The It Girl'?

8 Which silent star had a contract forbidding him to smile on screen?

9 Which silent film star became a father at the age of 73?

10 Which comedy star was the first screen performer to make $1 million a year — a) Charlie Chaplin b) Buster Keaton or c) Fatty Arbuckle?

11 What were the 3000 projectiles used in Laurel and Hardy's *Battle of the Century*?

12 Which bits of Charlie Chaplin were insured for $150 000?

13 Which bespectacled comedian gained fame for performing his own stunts?

14 What did the famous sign on the hills above Hollywood originally spell out?

15 Who was the star of the 1921 film *The Sheik*?

16 Which leading lady of the silent screen had a name that was an anagram of Arab Death?

17 Who was the silent star of the 1922 film *The Paleface*?

18 Who was the thin half of Laurel and Hardy?

19 Which silent film star lost part of his hand when a 'fake' bomb blew up?

20 In which hand did this star carry his cane?

(1) In which movie did this actor first play God?

(2) Does Adam have a navel, as portrayed in the 1966 movie *The Bible*?

(3) In which musical did Ted Neeley play Jesus?

(4) Who directed *The Ten Commandments*, *King of Kings* and *Samson and Delilah*, among other Biblical epics?

(5) Which 1951 Biblical epic starred Robert Taylor and Peter Ustinov?

6 Who was the star of *The Song of Bernadette*?

7 In which 1967 fantasy movie did John Phillip Law play a tarnished angel?

8 Who was the star of the 1978 movie *Heaven Can Wait*?

9 What role did Richard Pryor play in *In God We Trust*?

10 Who starred as the black Angel Levine?

11 In which movie did Rex Harrison persuade Charlton Heston to paint the ceiling of the Sistine Chapel?

12 In which movie was James Stewart saved from suicide by an elderly angel?

13 Who was the star of *The Nun's Story*?

14 In which 1968 movie did Anthony Quinn and John Gielgud play popes?

15 Whose only line in *The Greatest Story Ever Told* was 'Truly this man was the Son of God'?

16 Who played a parson in the 1963 film *Heavens Above*?

17 Who played Thomas à Becket in *Becket*?

18 Who played the priest in *Exorcist II*?

19 In which movie did Debbie Reynolds play a nun who takes her music into the world?

20 In which movie did Max von Sydow play Christ?

1 What was Walt Disney's first full-length feature cartoon?

2 Which Walt Disney character first appeared in 1934 in *The Wise Little Hen* with the words, 'Who — me? Oh no! I got a bellyache!'

3 Which Walt Disney film featured the song 'Never Smile At A Crocodile'?

4 Which Disney documentary features a shot of scorpions doing a square dance?

5 Which character was carved by Geppetto?

6 Which Disney cartoon film saw two animals eating spaghetti at Tony's restaurant?

7 What was Mickey Mouse's original name?

8 Which Disney character's voice was supplied by Clarence Nash?

9 What feature did Walt Disney sport that none of his employees is allowed to?

10 Which cartoon featured the song 'When You Wish Upon A Star'?

11 Which Robert Louis Stevenson story became Walt Disney's first non-animated film in 1950?

12 What was the name of the Volkswagen Beetle that starred in *The Love Bug*?

13 Which of the Seven Dwarfs doesn't have a beard?

14 How did Bambi's mother die?

15 Which Disney production featured music by Bach, Tchaikovsky, Stravinsky, Beethoven, Mussorgsky and Schubert?

16 Which Disney cartoon featured a song entitled 'Bibbidy Bobbidy Boo'?

17 In which film did Dick Van Dyke dance with animated penguins?

18 What was the name of Donald Duck's girlfriend?

19 Which Disney feature cartoon is about a boy called Wart who grows up to become King Arthur?

20 Which Disney character's figure was based on this actress's vital statistics?

1 Who made his first appearance in the cartoon *Steamboat Willie*?

2 Which 1954 thriller was the first to be based on a TV series?

3 Which was the first film shot in black and white to be converted to colour using a computer process?

4 Which movie was the last for Marilyn Monroe and Clark Gable?

5 Which 'bad guy' got his first break as a child advertising Mellin's babyfood?

6 What movie missiles were first perfected by Greenberg's patisserie and came in lemon and blackberry flavours?

7 What was John Wayne's last movie?

8 Who was the first American actress to appear on a postage stamp?

9 Which actress was the first to simulate the sex act in a feature film?

10 What was the first talking motion picture with the sound on the film?

11 Which Polish immigrant developed Supreme Greasepaint, the first make-up specially for the movies?

12 Which film star received her first screen kiss from Marshall Thompson at the age of 14 — a) Elizabeth Taylor b) Diana Dors or c) Judy Garland?

13 Who made his first recorded screen debut in *A Party at Kitty and Stud's*?

14   What was Richard Burton's last movie?

15   Which fashion item, first popularized by Greta Garbo in the thirties, was revived by Faye Dunaway's role in *Bonnie and Clyde*?

16   In which film were Humphrey Bogart and Lauren Bacall paired for the first time?

17   Which film presented this actor with his first starring role?

18   What was Steve McQueen's last movie?

19   Who was the first British monarch to be filmed?

20   What was the first of the Carry On series of movies — a) *Carry On Camping*   b) *Carry On Nurse* or c) *Carry On Sergeant*?

(1) What was this star's nickname?

(2) Which star was born Marion Morrison?

(3) What is the real surname of Diane Keaton, star of *Annie Hall*?

(4) What was Greta Gustafsson's stage name?

(5) What was 'Fatty' Arbuckle's real name?

(6) What was Marilyn Monroe's real name?

(7) Which actor took his name from a movie about a mutiny which starred Humphrey Bogart?

8 By what name was Julius Marx more commonly known?

9 Which actor is known as the Italian Stallion?

10 Which singer and actor got his stage name from a comic strip entitled *The Bingfield Bugle*?

11 Which craggy Hollywood star was named by his agent after Gibraltar and a river in New York?

12 Which actor became famous as the Man of a Thousand Faces?

13 What did British actor James Stewart decide to change his name to when he went to Hollywood?

14 Which brothers took their stage names from a comic strip entitled *Mager's Monks*?

15 Which actress was known as America's Sweetheart?

16 Which film star was known as the Handsomest Man in the World — a) Francis X. Bushman b) Rudolph Valentino or c) Errol Flynn?

17 Which actor chose to take the same name as a famous English explorer of Africa?

18 Which writer and comic film star was born Allen Stewart Konigsberg?

19 How are Louis Francis Cristillo and William Abbott better known?

20 Which film star began life in Bristol as Archibald Leach?

1 Which 1973 movie featured a corruption-fighting cop who walked a sheepdog called Alfie?

2 Which city's police force employed Dirty Harry?

3 Which police force did Mack Sennett create?

4 Which star of *Starsky and Hutch* played the part of a cop gone wrong in *Magnum Force*?

5 Which film pits Humphrey Bogart against gangsters in the Florida keys?

6 Which tough district of New York was the setting for the Paul Newman film *Fort Apache*?

7 In which movie did Robert de Niro play Al Pacino's father?

8 Who played the lead in *The Birdman of Alcatraz*?

9 What word was intentionally omitted from the screenplay of *The Godfather*?

10 Who starred as the businessman-turned-vigilante in *Death Wish*?

11 Which film has Steve McQueen and Dustin Hoffman imprisoned on Devil's Island?

12 What is the name of Inspector Clouseau's boss in the Pink Panther movies?

13 Who played the detective in *The Detective*?

14 Which fictional private eye features in *The Big Sleep*?

15 Which Hepburn starred in *How to Steal a Million* — Audrey or Katharine?

16 Who was the gangster star of *White Heat*?

17 Which 1971 thriller features Donald Sutherland as a policeman who gets involved with a call girl played by Jane Fonda?

18 Which gangster movie had Edward G. Robinson dying with the words, 'Mother of Mercy, is this the end of Rico'?

19 Who played a cop among the Amish in *Witness*?

20 What was this movie character's surname?

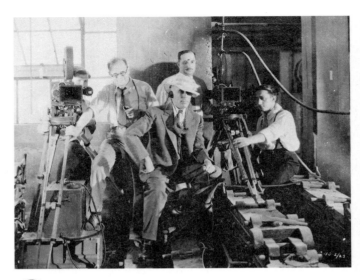

(1) Which movie mogul is this?

(2) Which 1956 religious film was Cecil B. de Mille's last?

(3) Which film company was founded by brothers Albert, Harry, Jack and Sam?

(4) Which sometime movie mogul made *Hell's Angels*?

(5) How many times was the gong struck at the beginning of J. Arthur Rank movies?

(6) Which movie boss was described as 'Czar of all the rushes'?

(7) Who was the only princess on the board of 20th Century Fox?

(8) Which film director and pioneer was responsible for the epic *The Birth of a Nation*?

(9) Which two movie moguls founded MGM?

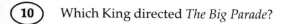

(10) Which King directed *The Big Parade*?

(11) Which film company was started in 1919 by Mary Pickford, Douglas Fairbanks, Charlie Chaplin and D. W. Griffith?

(12) With which surname did Samuel Goldwyn start life — a) Goldfinch b) Goldfish or c) Goldrush?

(13) Which producer was responsible for *Gone with the Wind* — a) Darryl F. Zanuck b) Irving Thalberg or c) David O. Selznick?

(14) Which studio was founded by a flour magnate intent on promoting religion?

(15) Which movie mogul is said to have said, 'A verbal contract isn't worth the paper it's written on'?

(16) Which movie mogul has a biography entitled *Don't Say Yes Until I Finish Talking'*?

(17) Which great director said, 'The length of a film should be directly related to the endurance of the human bladder'?

(18) Which British film studio was famous for its comedies, including *The Lavender Hill Mob*?

(19) Which movie company started out as a venture by the Radio Corporation of America and the Keith-Orpheum cinema circuit?

(20) Which film company is headed by Yoram Globus and Menahem Golan?

1 Where was Rick's Café?

2 In which 1951 musical did Gene Kelly play an American artist abroad?

3 In which 1977 movie did Liza Minnelli play a Hollywood star and Robert de Niro her saxophonist boyfriend?

4 Where did the 'beautiful blonde' played by Betty Grable come from?

5 Which movie featured Elvis Presley as a GI-turned-beachcomber?

6 Where did Dolly Parton keep a little whorehouse?

7 Which city did the dog Won Ton Ton save in 1976?

8 In which city did the American werewolf find himself in 1981?

9 Which Robert Altman film was set in the world's country music capital?

10 Which 1940 movie featured Sabu as a juvenile criminal?

11 What was the title of the second James Bond movie?

12 Which American city was destroyed in the 1973 movie *Earthquake*?

13 Which 1961 movie was about the sabotage of giant guns on a Turkish island?

14 In which 1979 Woody Allen movie did Mariel Hemingway star?

15 For which film did Dame Peggy Ashcroft receive her first Oscar?

16 In which movie did Orson Welles and Rita Hayworth star together?

17 Which historical movie featured Charlton Heston playing General Gordon?

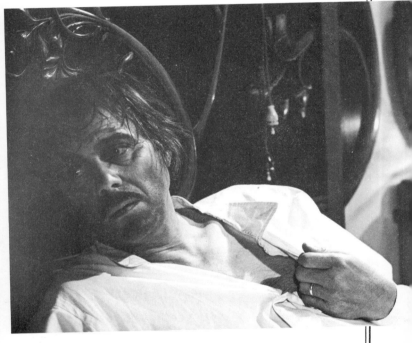

18 In which city did this actor meet his 'death' in 1971?

19 In which city was *Don't Look Now* filmed?

20 Where did Spencer Tracy, Marlene Dietrich, Burt Lancaster, Judy Garland and others go for trial?

1. In which country are the Mad Max movies made?

2. Which Polish director was responsible for *Man of Iron*?

3. Which German director created Marlene Dietrich's image, as well as directing her early films?

4. Which country has the world's largest movie output?

5. In which country was the 1947 classic *Bicycle Thieves* made?

6. Which classic French film is shown here?

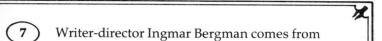

7 Writer-director Ingmar Bergman comes from which country?

8 Who wrote and directed *The Discreet Charm of the Bourgeoisie*?

9 Whose marriage did Rainer Werner Fassbinder direct in 1978?

10 Which French actor starred in the 1982 movie *Danton*?

11 Which director made *A Bout de Souffle*, translated as *Breathless*, in 1960?

12 What is the translation of the 1982 German World War II film *Das Boot*?

13 Which Russian director made the classic *Ivan the Terrible*?

14 Which Italian director filmed *Otello* in 1986?

15 Who wrote and directed the French comedy *Monsieur Hulot's Holiday*?

16 Film versions of which Bizet opera were offered by Peter Brook, Franco Rossi and Carlos Saura in 1984?

17 Which director made *Ran*?

18 Which German actress starred in the 1980 movie *Tess*?

19 What is the smallest country with an established movie output — a) Indonesia b) Iraq or c) Iceland?

20 Which director made *Fitzcarraldo*?

1 Who played the Cowardly Lion in *The Wizard of Oz*?

2 In which 1979 movie did Justin Henry play Meryl Streep's son?

3 Which actress was the female member of the 'Road' trio?

4 Which classic movie has Joseph Cotten, Everett Sloane and Agnes Moorehead among its supporting cast?

5 Which quintessentially British actor got his first break playing a Mexican in a western?

6 Who played Lex Luthor, Superman's arch-enemy, in *Superman?*

7 Which movie had an all-female cast and 135 speaking parts?

8 What was the name of Mickey Mouse's horsy friend, who appeared in cartoons in the thirties?

9 Who played the Master of Ceremonies at the Kit Kat Club in *Cabaret*?

10 In which classic Hitchcock movie did Judith Anderson play a sinister housekeeper?

11 Who played Sylvester Stallone's wife in the *Rocky* series?

12 For her performance as a maid in which movie did Hattie McDaniel become the first black performer to win an Oscar?

13 Who played movie sidekick to Hopalong Cassidy, Gene Autry, Roy Rogers and John Wayne?

14 Who played Inspector Clouseau's manic Chinese manservant in the Pink Panther movies?

15 In which film did Olivia De Havilland play Melanie Wilkes?

16 In which movie was this supporting actor paid $3 million for a ten-minute performance?

17 Which part did Tamara de Treaux play in *E. T.*?

18 In which movie did Josephine Hull and Jean Adair play Cary Grant's aunts?

19 Who portrayed the Bad in *The Good, the Bad and the Ugly*?

20 Who is the only girl to have appeared in two James Bond movies?

1. Which actor was responsible for this star's death in three different films?

2. Which 1978 'super' movie had end credits that ran for seven and a half minutes?

3. Whose self-penned epitaph read, 'On the whole, I'd rather be in Philadelphia'?

4. On which killer's story was *The Executioner's Song* based?

5. Which late American actor made his last screen appearance in *Ragtime*?

6. Who made her last film appearance in the uncompleted movie *Something's Got to Give*?

7 Which of James Dean's films was released after his death?

8 Which star's own epitaph read, 'He was an average guy who could carry a tune'?

9 Which actor died in a car crash while travelling west on Californian highway 466?

10 Which Blues Brother and National Lampoon actor died in 1983?

11 Which debonair British actor died of Motor Neurone Disease in 1983?

12 Who was posthumously awarded the 1976 Best Actor Oscar for *Network*?

13 Whose 'family' murdered Sharon Tate?

14 What was the murder weapon in *Dressed To Kill*?

15 Which movie star's last words are reputed to have been, 'I want you to believe I was driving'?

16 Which of Marilyn Monroe's husbands had red roses delivered to her grave every week?

17 Whose body was stolen from the cemetery at Corsier, Switzerland?

18 Whose death in 1926 caused a number of suicides among his fans?

19 Whose death inspired Dino de Laurentiis to say, 'Nobody cry when Jaws die, but when the monkey die, people gonna cry'?

20 What item of clothing was Marilyn Monroe wearing when she was found after her death?

1 Who coupled with Satan and gave birth to a little devil in a 1968 movie?

2 Which star began his horror film career in the 1953 movie *House of Wax*?

3 What was the name of Dr Frankenstein's hump-backed assistant?

4 According to Bram Stoker's novel, should actors playing Dracula have a moustache?

5 Which comedy star had his first major role in the 1939 spoof horror movie *The Cat and the Canary*?

6 Which actor was buried in Dracula's cloak?

7 Which 1984 horror movie has the subtitle *The Final Chapter*?

8 Which British film studio is famous for its low-budget horror movies?

9 Which character is most frequently portrayed in horror movies?

10 Which movie saw a little devil being born at 6 a.m. on the sixth day of the sixth month?

11 Who played Dracula in the spoof horror movie *Love at First Bite*?

12 Which British musician and multi-instrumentalist wrote the soundtrack for *The Exorcist*?

13 What must a human being be doing to be taken over by aliens in *Invasion of the Body Snatchers*?

14 What colour was Regan MacNeil's vomit in *The Exorcist*?

15 What character is the second most frequently portrayed in horror films?

16 Which film starring Sissy Spacek climaxed at the Bates High School senior prom?

17 Who is this horror star, who was born in Lugos, Hungary?

18 Which 1961 horror movie is set in the torture chamber of a Spanish castle?

19 What, according to Alfred Hitchcock, was used to represent blood in the shower scene in *Psycho*?

20 Which character from *Nightmare On Elm Street* comes back for revenge in the sequel?

(1) Who became the oldest director to make a major movie when he was signed to direct *Rich and Famous* at the age of 81?

(2) Who designed a special bra for Jane Russell?

(3) What were woven from human hair in 1916 to make film stars' eyes look bigger?

(4) Why did this movie have to be almost entirely re-shot for US audiences?

(5) Which MGM figure has been played by Spats, Jackie, Tanner and Jackie II?

(6) Which weighty comedian donated his trousers for Charlie Chaplin's tramp costume?

(7) For which movie did Nikki van der Zyl dub all Raquel Welch's Neanderthal grunts?

8 What did Gary Cooper, Frank Sinatra and Henry Fonda all have to improve their screen appearances?

9 Which mammoth role required John Hurt to spend seven hours a day being made up?

10 Which leading role did Norma Shearer claim she turned down?

11 Who demanded 342 takes of a silent scene in the 1931 film *City Lights*?

12 Which film was the first to feature earth-shaking Sensurround?

13 Which movie pioneer devised the 35mm gauge for film that is still used today?

14 Was the severed horse's head placed in the bed in *The Godfather* the real thing or a fake?

15 From what was the telephone that Harpo Marx ate in *The Cocoanuts* made?

16 Which John Huston movie required the props department to build 20 fake whales?

17 Which Michael Caine film was dubbed 127 times to make his speech comprehensible to US cinema audiences?

18 Who did 59 takes of a scene in *Some Like It Hot* in which her only line was, 'Where's the Bourbon'?

19 What were the boots that Charlie Chaplin ate in *The Gold Rush* made from?

20 In which of her movies did Elizabeth Taylor make a record 65 costume changes?

1 Which 'abominable' doctor was played by Vincent Price?

2 Who 'doesn't live here any more', according to Martin Scorsese's 1975 movie?

3 Who did Bette Davis tell us all about?

4 Which 1966 movie gave Michael Caine star status?

5 To which shy schoolteacher did we say goodbye in 1939 and 1969?

6 Which controversial Derek Jarman film had Latin dialogue?

7 Which of Daphne du Maurier's novels became a movie starring Laurence Olivier and Joan Fontaine?

8 Which film starred Mick Jagger as an Australian outlaw?

9 Which Swedish queen was played by Greta Garbo in 1933?

10 Which film featured James Mason as a middle-aged lecturer who falls in love with a 14-year-old girl?

11 What was the name of Roddy McDowell's equine friend in the 1943 family hit?

12 Who did Bob and Carol nearly swap with?

13 Which 1957 Debbie Reynolds film gave her a number one hit record?

14 Which Bette Davis movie was about a mad film star living with her crippled sister?

15 Who was a suitable case for treatment in 1966?

16 Which 'sister' was killed in a controversial 1969 movie?

17 Which American civil war melodrama features Bette Davis as a wilful southern belle who is reformed when plague strikes her town?

18 Which horror movie ended with a hand rising from the grave?

19 In which movie did James Stewart have an imaginary white rabbit as a friend?

20 In which movie did this star make her 1970 comeback?

1 How much were this actress's legs insured for — a) $1 million b) $5 million or c) $10 million?

2 Which Brazilian musical star's career hit rock bottom when photographs revealed that she didn't wear underwear while dancing?

3 Which singer played Nathan Detroit in the movie version of *Guys and Dolls*?

4 Which 1980 movie starred Olivia Newton-John as the reincarnated Greek muse Terpsichore?

5 In which film did Barbra Streisand first appear as Fanny Brice?

6 What was *the* film musical of 1965?

7 Which British movie, the first to be released in Red China, featured dancing pigs in Victorian costume?

8 Which 1983 hit movie, starring Irene Cara, sparked the popularity of breakdancing?

9 Which hoofer danced with a mouse in the film *Anchors Aweigh*?

10 Which American musical was based on the play *Green Grow the Rushes*?

11 Who danced with Carole Lombard in *Rumba* and *Bolero*?

12 Which 1949 musical featured the song 'Diamonds Are A Girl's Best Friend'?

13 In which 1978 movie did John Travolta play the part of Tony Manero?

14 Who showed her worth by dancing to stardom with Fred Astaire in the 1941 film *You'll Never Get Rich*?

15 What was mixed with water to make the rain show up better in Gene Kelly's big *Singin' in the Rain* number?

16 Who designed Ginger Roger's dresses in *The Story of Vernon and Irene Castle*?

17 Who is described in these screen test notes: 'Can't act. Can't sing. Can dance a little'?

18 Which musical featured the number 'Cheek To Cheek'?

19 Which Alan Parker movie spawned a successful TV series?

20 Which flop 1975 musical, starring Burt Reynolds, aimed to recreate the classic movies of the thirties?

1 Who plays the title role in the Mad Max movies?

2 Which English actor played the leading role in the 1940 production of *Pride and Prejudice*?

3 With which leading man did Vivien Leigh refuse to act unless he remedied the foul odour from his false teeth?

4 Which leading man was the original choice for James Bond?

5 Which actor played the 'female' musician Daphne in *Some Like It Hot*?

6 In which country was Rudolph Valentino born?

7 Which leading man has published three novels, including *West of Sunset*?

8 Which two Anthonys starred in *The Guns of Navarone*?

9 How much was Dustin Hoffman paid for playing *Tootsie* — a) $1 million b) $2 million or c) $4 million?

10 Which American comedian made his movie comeback in *The Sunshine Boys*?

11 Which leading man's first act as mayor of Carmel was to legalize ice cream parlours?

12 Who was Barbra Streisand's leading man in *Funny Girl*?

13 Which British actor was nicknamed The Thinking Woman's Crumpet?

14 Which of Hollywood's current leading men won the Mr Universe competition five times?

15 Who was this actress's leading man in the 1985 movie *Falling in Love*?

16 Who played the leading character, Hickey, in *The Iceman Cometh*?

17 Which tough guy's last film was *The Harder They Fall* in 1956?

18 Which leading actor is father of Brat Pack hero Emilio Estevez?

19 Which leading man had ears that, according to Howard Hughes, made him look like 'a taxicab with both doors open'?

20 Who was the biggest male box office attraction in 1980?

1 Which of these Marx Brothers was born first — a) Chico b) Harpo or c) Groucho?

2 Which actress is the daughter of Charlie Chaplin and grandaughter of playwright Eugene O'Neill?

3 To which famous author are actresses Margaux and Mariel related?

4 Who is 'scream queen' Jamie Lee Curtis's father?

5 Who was Rita Hayworth's first cousin — a) Katharine Hepburn b) Ginger Rogers or c) Doris Day?

6 To which member of the British royal family is this actor distantly related?

7 Which Italian actress is the sister of Mussolini's daughter-in-law?

8 Into which famous American family did Arnold Schwarzenneger marry?

9 Which father and daughter team starred in the 1973 movie *Paper Moon*?

10 Who is Warren Beatty's famous sister?

11 Who is Professor Ludwig von Drake's feathered nephew?

12 What was the sixth Marx Brother called —
a) Nico b) Frenchie or c) there wasn't one?

13 Which father and son won Oscars for *The Treasure of the Sierra Madre*?

14 What relation was the canine star of *The Magic of Lassie*, made in 1977, to the original star of *Lassie Come Home*, made in 1942?

15 Who are Sir Michael Redgrave's two acting daughters?

16 Which film and soap star is the son of Mary Martin?

17 Which star of *A Room with a View* is the great-great-niece of British Prime Minister Herbert Asquith?

18 Which father and daughter appeared together in *On Golden Pond*?

19 Who is Debbie Reynolds' daughter, the female star of the *Star Wars* trilogy?

20 Who was Liza Minnelli's mother?

1 Which two movies, one starring Sherlock Holmes and the other Michael Caine, share the same title?

2 Which film cast Clint Eastwood in the role of a radio disc jockey with a murderous fan?

3 Which Alfred Hitchcock movie starred Julie Andrews?

4 Which 1974 whodunnit had more than twelve stars in its cast?

5 How did Donald Sutherland's child die in *Don't Look Now*?

6 Who played the title character in *The Day of the Jackal*?

7 Which Hitchcock movie was about a woman going missing on a train journey from Switzerland to England?

8 What is the connection between the movie *Death on the Nile* and British aristocrat Lady Mallowan?

9 Which airborne suspense film starred Burt Lancaster, Dean Martin and Jacqueline Bisset?

10 Which classic murder mystery starred William Powell as a tipsy detective and Myrna Loy as his wife?

11 Which John Buchan thriller has been filmed three times with, respectively, Robert Donat, Kenneth More and Robert Powell in the starring role?

12 Which 1974 thriller had Jon Voight stalking the Butcher of Riga?

13 In which Hitchcock movie did this star stab her assailant with a pair of scissors?

14 What part did Humphrey Bogart play in *The Maltese Falcon*?

15 Who was the star of the 1974 murder mystery *Chinatown*?

16 In which European city is *The Third Man* set?

17 Who was the female star of *The Spiral Staircase*?

18 In which movie did Jack Nicholson deliver the spine-chilling line, 'H-e-e-e-re's Johnny!'?

19 Who was the female lead in the 1975 remake of *Farewell My Lovely*?

20 Which spellbinding 1945 movie starred Ingrid Bergman and Gregory Peck in a mental institution?

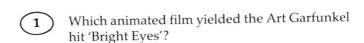

1. Which animated film yielded the Art Garfunkel hit 'Bright Eyes'?

2. Who composed the theme music for *Jaws*?

3. Which movie classic introduced 'Tara's Theme'?

4. Which movie had 'The Entertainer' as its theme tune?

5. Who composed the title song for this movie?

6. Who composed the theme music for *Chariots of Fire*?

7. What was the Oscar-winning theme song of *Breakfast at Tiffany's*?

8. Who wrote and had a hit with the title song from *Footloose*?

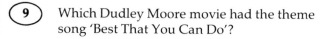

9 Which Dudley Moore movie had the theme song 'Best That You Can Do'?

10 Which 1972 film included a scene and a theme tune that led to a boom in the sales of banjos?

11 Who had a hit with the film theme song 'Against All Odds'?

12 Which band provided the theme song for *Pretty in Pink*?

13 Who was commissioned to write the theme tune for *Star Wars*?

14 Which Palm D'Or winner at the Cannes Film Festival had its theme music written by Ennio Morricone?

15 Who sang the theme song for *Born Free*?

16 For which of the movies in which she starred did Barbra Streisand write 'Evergreen'?

17 For which James Bond movie did Nancy Sinatra sing the theme song?

18 Who sang the theme song for *Absolute Beginners*?

19 Which movie had the theme song 'Stayin' Alive'?

20 Which Rocky movie opened with 'Eye Of The Tiger'?

1 How did Warren Beatty whizz around in *Shampoo*?

2 Which choo-choo was serenaded in *Sun Valley Serenade*?

3 Which shipping disaster was featured in *A Night to Remember* in 1958?

4 Which female flying ace's film biography is called *They Flew Alone*?

5 What form of air transport was used to start the journey in *Around the World in Eighty Days*?

6 What was the Silver Streak in the 1976 Gene Wilder film?

7 Which Marx Brothers movie has a hilarious scene in the cabin of an ocean liner?

8 Which actor was chased through a field by an aeroplane in *North by Northwest?*

9 In which Beatles movie do the Fab Four travel from Liverpool to London on a train?

10 Who performed Steve McQueen's motorcycle stunts in *The Great Escape*?

11 What kind of car did Bullitt drive?

12 On which river did *Showboat* sail?

13 Which railroad was celebrated in an Oscar-winning song in *The Harvey Girls*?

14 Who was the *Girl on a Motorcycle*?

15 What make of gadget-laden car did James Bond drive in *Goldfinger*?

16 Which motorcycle movie featured Peter Fonda, Dennis Hopper and Jack Nicholson?

17 What was the *Twentieth Century* in the movie of the same name?

18 What make of motorcycle did Marlon Brando ride in *The Wild One*?

19 Which make of Ford was most often used by Laurel and Hardy?

20 What make of car did this film character drive?

▼

(1) In which Bond film did this actress emerge from the sea wearing a white bikini?

(2) Which was the most commercially successful James Bond movie — a) *Goldfinger* b) *From Russia with Love* or c) *Thunderball*?

(3) What was the nickname of the Bond adversary with metal teeth?

(4) Which actor played James Bond in *On Her Majesty's Secret Service*?

5 Which dapper actor was Ian Fleming's own choice to play James Bond?

6 Who sang the theme song for *Diamonds Are Forever*?

7 Which Bond movie was Roger Moore's first?

8 Which of James Bond's adversaries had bionic hands?

9 How does James Bond like his Martini made?

10 Which stronghold did Goldfinger plan to relieve of its gold?

11 Which Bond movie pits 007 against voodoo and a black master criminal?

12 What was the first James Bond movie?

13 Which evil organization does 007 fight?

14 For which James Bond movie was Burt Bacharach's 'The Look Of Love' written?

15 Who did Bernard Lee play in the Bond films?

16 Which actress played Pussy Galore?

17 Who does M's typing and filing?

18 In which 1985 movie did Sean Connery make his 'Bond' comeback?

19 Who was named as the new James Bond in 1986?

20 What is the name of Bond's fearsome bowler-hatted adversary in *Goldfinger*?

1   Who played the part of the aging Mrs Moore in *A Passage to India*?

2   Who played the outlaw Josey Wales?

3   Who played Clyde in *Bonnie and Clyde*?

4   Who played all eight leading roles in *Kind Hearts and Coronets*?

5   Who played Randall McMurphy in *One Flew Over The Cuckoo's Nest*?

6   Which famous movie star was played by Jerry Lacey in *Play It Again, Sam*?

7   Who played Tarzan in more films than anyone else?

8   Who played the part of the waitress who falls in love with Arthur in *Arthur*?

9   Who played the title role in 1939's *Beau Geste*?

10   Who starred in the film *The Eiger Sanction*?

11   Who played Gladys Aylward in *The Inn of the Sixth Happiness*?

12   Who played the young lead in *Back to the Future*?

13   Who played Maria in the movie version of *West Side Story*?

14   Who played the part of a missionary in *Shanghai Surprise*?

15   Who played George Webber in *10*?

16   Who played Ratzo in *Midnight Cowboy*?

17 Who rose to international fame playing this part?

18 Who played Thomas, the photographer, in *Blow Up*?

19 Who played Doris Day's husband in *Move Over Darling*?

20 Who played Rufus T. Firefly in *Duck Soup*?

1 For which movie did Dr Haing S. Ngor win a Best Supporting Actor Oscar?

2 Which 1972 film marked Diana Ross's movie debut?

3 Which non-actress turned down a $1 million offer to play opposite Anthony Quinn in *The Greek Tycoon*?

4 In which feature film did this rock singer make her screen debut?

5 Which of Elizabeth Taylor's ex-husbands appeared as a fisherman in *The Mirror Crack'd*?

6 Which far eastern prince directed *Storm Over Angkor*?

7 Which thrilling male singer starred in *The Wiz*?

8 Which left-wing South African playwright appeared as right-wing General Jan Smuts in *Gandhi*?

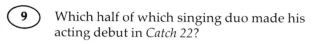

9 Which half of which singing duo made his acting debut in *Catch 22*?

10 Which member of the Princess of Wales's family had a bit part in *Another Country*?

11 Which Australian prime minister played a man in a bar in *Barry McKenzie Holds His Own*?

12 Which singer starred with Jane Fonda and Lily Tomlin in *9 to 5*?

13 Which founder of the Playboy empire appeared as an ancient Roman in *History of the World — Part I*?

14 Which singer starred in *Purple Rain*?

15 Which author took a bit part in the movie of his novel *The Old Man and the Sea*?

16 Which Boomtown Rat starred in the Pink Floyd movie *The Wall*?

17 Which aging rock star played an aging rock star in *Performance*?

18 Which American ex-president's wife had walk-on parts in *Becky Sharp* and *Small Town Girl*?

19 Which ballet dancer turned to acting in *White Knights*?

20 What character does body-builder Dave Prowse play in the *Star Wars* trilogy?

1 Which war movie co-starred Richard Burton and Clint Eastwood?

2 Which actor led the attack on the bridge on the River Kwai?

3 Which British movie was about Dr Barnes Wallis and his damn bouncing bombs?

4 Who played the Greek resistance fighter Andrea Stavros in *The Guns of Navarone*?

5 Which war provided the setting for *The Red Badge of Courage*?

6 Which movie, starring Michael Caine, was about a German plot to kill Winston Churchill in England?

7 Who played Colonel Mike Kirby in the Vietnam war movie *The Green Berets*?

8 Which 1963 movie had Steve McQueen as a prisoner of war attempting to jump over a barbed wire fence?

9 Which movie set Michael Caine in the Battle of Rorke's Drift?

10 In which movie did Jon Voight play a disabled Vietnam veteran who has an affair with Jane Fonda?

11 *Oh What a Lovely War* was about which war?

12 What are Darth Vader's troops called?

13 Who played Hawkeye Pearce in the movie version of *M*A*S*H*?

14 Which game kills Christopher Walken in *The Deer Hunter*?

15 What was the Blue Max in the film *The Blue Max*?

16 Who appeared as the mad Colonel in *Apocolypse Now*?

17 Which war provides the setting for *The Good, the Bad and the Ugly*?

18 Into which country did the Dirty Dozen parachute?

19 In which country did Ronald Reagan find himself a *Prisoner of War* in 1954?

20 What is this officer's rank?

1 Which of this actress's films was a favourite of Adolf Hitler?

2 Which Oscar-winning movie was shown at the 1981 Royal Command Performance?

3 Which country bans the public presentation of films for being contrary to Islamic belief?

4 What name was given to a Liverpool cinema opened in 1914 — a) the Cabbage b) the Carrot or c) the Onion?

5 Which Russian leader was, according to Kruschev, particularly fond of watching westerns?

6 Who received more fan mail during their years of popularity — Shirley Temple or Mickey Mouse?

7 The first cinema in Peking to show talkies was called the Peace and Quiet — true or false?

8 In which European capital was the first cinema opened?

9 How many projectors were used to put Cinerama movies on the screen?

10 Which two French brothers first set the world of film and cinema alight?

11 Where was the premiere of the 1940 movie *Dodge City* held?

12 Which recent American president was enrolled as a member of the Errol Flynn Fan Club?

13 Which airline was the first to show regular in-flight movies — a) Pan Am b) Aeroflot or c) TWA?

14 Which long-distance train was the first to have movies shown on board?

15 Which character's films are shown at the Camera cinema in Berlin and the Kolosseum Kino in Vienna to the exclusion of all others?

16 Which country had a cinema first — a) Iran b) Iceland or c) Greece?

17 Who got most fan mail in 1928 — Charlie Chaplin or Rin Tin Tin?

18 What was the name of the largest cinema ever built — a) the Regal b)the Miramar or c) the Roxy?

19 Which country had the most cinemas in 1984 — a) Chile b) Ghana or c) Israel?

20 Outside which cinema has it become traditional for film stars to leave their footprints in cement?

1 In which 'reflective' movie did Marlon Brando, playing Elizabeth Taylor's husband, become obsessed with a male soldier?

2 What colour was Betty, according to a 1986 movie?

3 What colour was the woman wearing in the 1948 adaptation of a Wilkie Collins novel?

4 What colour was Audie Murphy's 'courageous badge'?

5 In which 'Beatles' movie did the Beatles not appear?

6 Which of Stanley Kubrick's movies went like 'clockwork'?

7 What colour was Woody Allen's Egyptian rose?

8 In which 1954 thriller did Spencer Tracy have a 'bad day'?

9 What 'colour' movie was based on Alice Walker's most famous novel?

10 In which 1952 Charlie Chaplin movie did the spotlight fall on Claire Bloom?

11 In which movie have Leslie Howard and David Niven played Sir Percy Blakeney?

12 What kind of bird was Shirley Temple searching for in a 1940 movie?

13 What colour was the fuzzy nightgown in the title of a Jane Russell movie?

14 Who 'wore black' in the title of a 1967 movie?

15 In which two 'blue' movies did this rock star appear?

16 Which 1968 movie about rebellion in an English public school alternates randomly between monochrome and colour?

17 What colour sky hung over a 1948 western starring Gregory Peck?

18 What colour coat was worn by the dwarf in *Don't Look Now*?

19 Which Dracula movie was the first black horror film?

20 Which Judy Garland movie had some scenes in full colour and others in sepia?

1 Which Marx Brothers movie centres on a stolen painting?

2 Which movie, set in New York in 1929, had gangster Fat Sam fighting it out with Dandy Dan?

3 In which movie did Robert Redford return from lunch to find his colleagues murdered?

4 Which movie doesn't show the face of leading man Claude Rains until the closing seconds?

5 What was this movie character's occupation before she went to work for the Von Trapp family?

6 Which 1949 film's climax took place in the Vienna sewer system?

7 Which movie features Donald Sutherland masquerading as a general inspecting troops?

8 Which movie is about war refugees waiting for American visas in a north African cafe?

9 Which sci-fi movie had aliens sending the coordinates 104-44-30-40-36-10 to Earth?

10 Which movie was about a gay bank robber trying to finance a sex-change operation for his lover?

11 In which movie did Peter Finch play a homosexual Jewish doctor whose lover was having an affair with Glenda Jackson?

12 In which movie did David Niven take his manservant, Cantinflas, on a long voyage?

13 Which 1963 movie starred Dirk Bogarde as a sinister manservant who gradually takes over from his master?

14 In which movie did Laurence Olivier torture Dustin Hoffman with a dentist's drill?

15 In which movie did twelve-year-old Leo run messages between Alan Bates and Julie Christie?

16 Which 1969 film was about an Edinburgh schoolmistress who proves to be a bad influence on her pupils?

17 Which 1971 movie concerned the seizure of 120lbs of pure heroin?

18 In which children's film did Benny Hill bang out toys as a toymaker?

19 Which movie included a scene in which Paul Newman ate fifty hard-boiled eggs?

20 Which daring war adventure is about a group of paratroopers dropped into the Alps to rescue an officer from an impregnable castle?

1 Which writer was played by Meryl Streep in *Out of Africa*?

2 Who was the female star of *9½ Weeks*?

3 Who played the girl in Peter Sellers's soup?

4 Who was Robert Redford's leading lady in *The Great Gatsby*?

5 Which actress stars as Ripley in *Aliens*?

6 About which female star did Louis B. Mayer say, 'She can't talk. She can't act. She's terrific'?

7 Who played Ilsa Lund Laszlo in *Casablanca*?

8 Who was silent star John Gilbert's most famous lover and co-star?

9 Which leading lady served a month in a Rome gaol in 1982 for income tax evasion?

10 Who played Dr Zhivago's mistress?

11 Which actress-turned-photojournalist scooped an interview with Fidel Castro?

12 Who played the part of the woman in the 1956 movie *And God Created Woman*?

13 Which living legend of the silver screen wrote a book entitled *Nibbles and Me*?

14 To whom is Anne Bancroft married?

15 Which famous role was auditioned for by 1400 actresses, and who got the part?

16 Which British actress played both title roles in 1982's *Victor/Victoria*?

17 Who was scheduled to play the lead in Hitchcock's *Marnie,* until the citizens of Monaco objected?

18 Which leading lady's bosom is this?

19 Who was known as the Professional Virgin?

20 Which actress was originally intended to play the lead in *The Wizard of Oz*?

1 Which Hollywood star was Erin Fleming accused of mistreating?

2 Which actress aired her staunch beliefs about adultery, then noted, 'That does not mean I don't pet with Carlo'?

3 What age will both Burt Reynolds and Woody Allen reach in 1995?

4 Who took Lee Marvin to court in the celebrated 'palimony' case of 1979?

5 Which film star was accused of raping Denise Duvivier on the day he married Patrice Wyman?

6 Which American actor served six months in Reading Gaol in 1984–85 for attempting to smuggle cocaine into Britain?

7 For whom did this star leave her husband and cause a long-lasting scandal?

8 Which movie star won the 1985 Sports Car Club of America National Championships?

9 Which star of *Pandora's Box* and other movies of the 1920s became a salesgirl at Saks Fifth Avenue?

10 Which female star of the sixties drowned in 1981?

11 Who was sentenced to 10 days' imprisonment after writing a play called *Sex*?

12 Which red-haired star of the silent screen painted her car and dyed her dogs to match?

13 Which movie was Grace Kelly making in Monaco when she met Prince Rainier?

14 What was Richard Burton referring to when he said, 'Apocalyptic — they would topple empires'?

15 What name did Douglas Fairbanks and Mary Pickford give to their Hollywood mansion?

16 Who sang 'Happy Birthday' to President John F. Kennedy at Madison Square Gardens in 1962?

17 Which silent star married a succession of teenage brides, causing a succession of scandals?

18 Who said of Steve McQueen that he didn't like the women in his life to have balls?

19 Who had her 1936 Miss Hungary title taken away because she was under age?

20 Which showbiz marriage was headlined in the press, 'Egghead weds Hourglass'?

1 Which Mel Brooks spoof used footage of Indians taken from the western *Hondo*?

2 Which actor in *The Magnificent Seven* portrayed the gunslinger who'd lost his nerve?

3 What was the sequel to *A Fistful of Dollars*?

4 Who was faster on the draw — Butch Cassidy or the Sundance Kid?

5 Which western's climax took place on the main street of Hadleyville on a Sunday?

6 Which country produced the first western to be filmed in colour?

7 Which Japanese film served as the basis for *The Magnificent Seven*?

8 Who played the part of the Ringo Kid in the original *Stagecoach* movie?

9 Which star of westerns died on 3 July 1965 at the age of 33, and was promptly stuffed?

10 What's the collective name for Italian-made western movies?

11 Which 1969 movie became the highest-grossing western of all time?

12 Which very unlikely star slipped off her mink coat to appear in *Johnny Guitar* in 1954?

13 Which classic western opens with a sign reading, 'Welcome to Bottleneck'?

14 On which wild west heroine's life is *Annie Get Your Gun* based?

15 Who was voted the most popular western star from 1943–54 inclusive?

16 Which 1970 western featured Dustin Hoffman as a veteran of the wild west who'd been raised as an Indian?

17 In which movie did Marlene Dietrich sing 'See What The Boys In The Back Room Will Have'?

18 Who played Buffalo Bill in *The Life of Buffalo Bill*, made in 1909?

19 Which western starred Richard Harris as an aristocratic Englishman captured by the Indians?

20 From which movie was this still taken?

(1) Who wrote the book on which this movie was based?

(2) Which Agatha Christie story gave Ingrid Bergman an Oscar-winning role in 1974?

(3) Which novel and consequent film made Peter Blatty a multi-millionaire?

(4) Which author has had the most films made of his works — a) Graham Greene b) Ernest Hemingway or c) William Shakespeare?

(5) Which of Daphne du Maurier's novels became Alfred Hitchcock's first Hollywood production?

(6) Which science fiction film was the first to be based on the book *The Sentinel*?

7 Which novel by Judith Rossner was made into a film starring Diane Keaton?

8 Which movie does author Ken Kesey refuse to watch?

9 Which Stanley Kubrick film, starring Jack Nicholson, was adapted from a Stephen King novel?

10 Which autobiographical movie of 1977 was based on the book *Pentimento* by Lillian Hellman?

11 Which epic, penned by Lew Wallace, has become a classic in both its film versions?

12 Who is the author of *The Three Musketeers* and *The Count of Monte Cristo*, whose works have been filmed 118 times?

13 Which fictional detective has become the character most often portrayed on screen?

14 Who wrote the novel *Frankenstein*?

15 Who wrote the novel and screenplay for *Love Story*?

16 Which crime writer invented the character of Philip Marlowe?

17 Whose stories formed the basis of Walt Disney's *The Jungle Book*?

18 Which fishy blockbusters were based on a Peter Benchley novel?

19 Which Paul Gallico novel about an overturned ship was made into a 1972 movie?

20 Who wrote *Around the World in Eighty Days*?

1 How many 'just' men were there?

2 How did Dudley Moore rate Bo Derek?

3 Who was the girl in *One Hundred Men and a Girl*?

4 How many dinosaurs went missing in a 1975 Walt Disney feature?

5 How many did Francis Ford Coppola give from the heart?

6 Who didn't skate on thin ice with the successful *One in a Million*?

7 How many coins were in the fountain in the 1954 movie?

8 How many brides and brothers were there altogether in the 1954 movie?

9 On which street did Ginger Rogers and Ruby Keeler dance in the 1933 film of the musical?

10 How many faces did Eve have, as played by Joanne Woodward in 1957?

11 How many feathers were received by the hero of a 1939 movie about heroism in the Sudan?

12 How many years did Spencer Tracy and Bette Davis spend in Sing Sing?

13 Which Welsh poet was one of the writers of *The Three Weird Sisters*?

14 How many bridges did Tony Curtis cross in a 1955 movie?

15 How many mules did Sister Sara have?

16 In which 'irritable' movie did Tom Ewell have a fling with Marilyn Monroe?

17 In which movie did John Hurt star as Winston Smith?

18 How many steps were taken in this movie?

19 Which number provided the title of Federico Fellini's 1963 movie?

20 How many little Indians were there in the title of a 1966 movie based on an Agatha Christie whodunnit?

1 Who is the only Hollywood leading lady of the last decade publicly to declare her virginity?

2 Which character was featured in a 1976 porno film and billed with the line, 'It's not his nose that grows'?

3 How big is the chest of Chesty Morgan, American sex star — a) 53 b) 63 or c) 73 inches?

4 Who buttered up this actress in *Last Tango in Paris*?

5 Which area of the USA has the highest concentration of sex cinemas — a) Los Angeles b) the Bible Belt or c) New York?

6 Which 1974 Sylvia Kristel film was artistically described as being an acceptable shade of blue?

7 Which founder of *Penthouse* was responsible for *Caligula*?

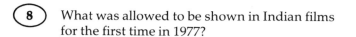

8 What was allowed to be shown in Indian films for the first time in 1977?

9 Which much-banned film was described by one critic as 'Hard to swallow'?

10 Which film version of a D. H. Lawrence novel became famous for its male nude wrestling scene?

11 Who was replaced from the neck down by Penthouse Pet Victoria Lynn Johnson for the shower scene of *Dressed to Kill*?

12 Which of Charlie Chaplin's films was banned for 20 years because he was believed to be too left-wing?

13 What was the first X-rated full length feature cartoon?

14 Is kissing allowed in Turkish movies?

15 Which is the only European country never to have exercised censorship of adult films?

16 What does the rating PG on films stand for?

17 What was the first X-rated film to win the Best Picture Oscar?

18 Who was the first star to be banned from the screen, despite being acquitted of the manslaughter of Virginia Rappe?

19 Which 1930 censorship code was named after the President of the Motion Picture Producers and Distributors of America?

20 Who was the only man in Germany to watch Chaplin's banned film *The Great Dictator* twice?

(1) Which 1970 tear-jerker had Jenny saying, 'I want you to be a merry widower'?

(2) Which 1954 film featured the line, 'I coulda been a contenda'?

(3) Which Robert Redford/Paul Newman film ended with the line, 'I'd just blow it'?

(4) Which movie ends with the line, 'After all, tomorrow is another day'?

(5) Which normally taciturn actor's most famous line is, 'Go on punk, make my day'?

(6) Which movie featured the line, 'Take a good look, old man. I'm Buck Barrow'?

(7) Which Hitchcock chiller included the line, 'A boy's best friend is his mother'?

(8) In which movie did Groucho Marx say, 'One morning I shot an elephant in my pajamas. How he ever got in my pajamas I'll never know'?

(9) Which Woody Allen movie warned, 'Be on the lookout for a large female breast, about a 4000 with an X cup'?

(10) Which movie contained the line, 'Of all the gin joints in all the towns in all of the world, she walks into mine'?

(11) Which 1968 movie included the line, 'He was a model for all of us, a gorilla to remember'?

(12) Which movie opened with the line, 'Last night I dreamt I went to Manderley again'?

(13) Which screen character declared, 'I never drink when I fly'?

14 Which film offered the line, 'The ship's company will remember that I am your captain, your judge and your jury'?

15 Which movie featured the line, 'Open the pod bay door, Hal'?

16 Which 1954 musical closed with the line, 'I now pronounce you men and wives'?

17 Which 1951 Brando film had Vivien Leigh pleading, 'I don't want realism — I want magic'?

18 In which film did Peter Lorre say to Humphrey Bogart, 'You will please clasp your hands together at the back of your neck'?

19 Who said, 'Beulah, peel me a grape'?

20 What did this actor never say in a movie?

1 Who, according to Groucho Marx, did he know before she was a virgin?

2 Of which Elizabeth Taylor epic flop did the director say, 'This picture was conceived in a state of emergency, shot in confusion and wound up in blind panic'?

3 Of whom was it said, 'She really ought to be called Barbra Strident'?

4 Which sex symbol was described by a make-up artist as, 'silicone from the knees up'?

5 Which dance star was described as, 'The nearest we are ever likely to get to a human Mickey Mouse'?

6 Of which writer, director and movie star was it said, 'There but for the grace of God, goes God'?

7 Who said, when asked what it was like to film a love scene with Marilyn Monroe, 'It's like kissing Hitler'?

8 Which comedienne described this actress as having, 'More chins than a Chinese phone book'?

9 Of which busty actress did Howard Hughes say, 'There are two good reasons why men go to see her. Those are enough'?

10 About whose performance in the play *The Lake* did Dorothy Parker say, 'She ran the gamut of emotions from A to B'?

11 Which of his female co-stars did Laurence Olivier describe as, 'A professional amateur'?

12 Of which famous tough guy was it said, 'Most of the time it sounds like he has a mouth full of wet toilet paper'?

13 Which silent star said of herself, 'I'm as pure as the driven slush'?

14 Which star of *On the Waterfront* said of himself, 'I have eyes like those of a dead pig'?

15 Who said, 'The best time I had with Joan Crawford was when I pushed her down the stairs in *Whatever Happened to Baby Jane*?

16 Which comedian, on meeting Greta Garbo, said, 'Excuse me, I thought you were a fellow I once knew in Pittsburgh'?

17 Of which legendary star was it said, 'Boiled down to essentials she is a plain girl with large feet'?

18 Who is reported to have said, 'Actors are cattle'?

19 Who was dubbed 'QE3' before shedding forty pounds for Broadway in 1981?

20 Of which dancing pair was it said, 'He gives her class and she gives him sex'?

(1) What athletic event was this star aiming at in the movie from which this still was taken?

(2) What sport was the subject of the movie *The Hustler*?

(3) Which Oscar-winning movie concerned the exploits of two Olympic runners?

(4) Which sport has had the most feature films made about it?

(5) Which sport was central to the Paul Newman movie *Somebody Up There Likes Me*?

(6) Which 1979 film about the tennis circuit starred Guillermo Vilas and John McEnroe?

7 Who won an Oscar for his portrayal of Jake La Motta in *Raging Bull*?

8 Who played Grand National winner Bob Champion in the movie *Champions*?

9 Which movie, starring James Caan, is about an ultra-violent game developed in the 21st century to entertain the masses?

10 Which sport is central to the Paul Newman film *Slap Shot*?

11 In which boxing movie did heavyweight champion Joe Frazier appear?

12 Which Indian tennis player appeared in the 1983 James Bond film *Octopussy*?

13 Who played Muhammad Ali in *The Greatest*, the 1977 story of his life?

14 At which sport was Robert Redford a natural in *The Natural*?

15 Who played Dr Hugo Z. Hackenbush in the 1937 movie *A Day at the Races*?

16 Which star put her three Olympic gold ice-skating medals to good use in her movies?

17 Which rags-to-riches film knocked out all competitors to win the 1976 Best Picture Oscar?

18 Which sport did film star Esther Williams excel at?

19 What sport does *Gregory's Girl* tackle?

20 Which 'sport' was featured in *Pumping Iron*?

1 Which movie scooped seven Oscars in 1986?

2 Which two British sisters were nominated for Best Actress Oscars in 1966?

3 Which 1950 Bette Davis movie won seven Oscars, including the one for Best Picture?

4 Who, in 1975, became the oldest actor to win an Oscar?

5 Who in his lifetime won more Oscars than any other person?

6 For which movie did Henry Fonda win his Oscar?

7 Which actress has received the most Oscar nominations?

8 Which famous concert did Michael Wadleigh film to win the 1970 Best Documentary Oscar?

9 For his performance in which 1968 film did John Wayne win an Oscar?

10 Who won an Oscar for skippering *The African Queen*?

11 Which actor was awarded an Oscar engraved in the name of Dick Tracy?

12 Which film won Marlon Brando the Oscar that he refused?

13 Who was the youngest actress ever to receive an Oscar?

14 Which British theatrical knight won an Oscar playing alongside Dudley Moore in *Arthur*?

15 Which is the only sequel to have won a Best Film Oscar?

16 Who won her second Oscar for her part in *Who's Afraid of Virginia Wolf*?

17 For which movie did this actor win his 1985 Best Actor Oscar?

18 Who is the only person to have won Oscars for Best Actress and Best Song?

19 Who won an Oscar for his portrayal of King Mon Kut?

20 Who won the Best Actor Oscar for his portrayal of Popeye Doyle?

1 Who inspired a fashion for women's trousers after her appearance in *Morocco*?

2 Which shoe featured in the title of a 1976 remake of the Cinderella story?

3 Which star of *Chanel Solitaire* insisted on her costumes being designed by Givenchy?

4 Which 1979 movie inspired a fashion for plaited and beaded hair?

5 Which star was famous for her overpadded shoulders, which sloped upwards from her neck?

6 In which movie did this actress play a model and fashion designer?

7 Which star of *Jungle Princess* inspired a fashion for sarongs?

8 What was Myrna Loy the first woman to wear on screen in *What Price Beauty*?

9 What kind of hat did Sherlock Holmes traditionally wear?

10 Who took off his shirt in *It Happened One Night* to reveal a bare chest — and sent sales of undershirts plummeting?

11 Which star of a 1960 movie set in the far east inspired a fashion for the cheongsam?

12 Who designed the costumes for *My Fair Lady*?

13 In which movie did Marlon Brando wear what has become standard leather biker's uniform?

14 What was the only part of Charlie Chaplin's tramp costume that he supplied himself?

15 Who was the star of *Baby Takes a Bow*, whose dress designs were marketed by her film studio?

16 Which Jane Fonda movie inspired a vogue for thigh-high vinyl boots?

17 Which bald star wore black for the last 45 years of his life?

18 How, according to a 1941 Errol Flynn movie, did they die?

19 Which singer and actress inspired a 1985 fashion for bare midriffs and tarty fashions?

20 Which leading character in a Woody Allen movie established a fashion for big, baggy clothing?

1 Which movie character has been played by Cesar Romero, Gilbert Rowland and Duncan Renaldo?

2 What was the name of E. T.'s best friend?

3 Which character did Rhett Butler pay $150 for a dance in *Gone with the Wind*?

4 In which movie did Michael Caine play the part of Dr Robert Elliott?

5 Which movie cast Humphrey Bogart in the role of Rick Blaine?

6 Which was Basil Rathbone's most famous screen character?

7 Which film character do the Japanese know as Mr Kiss Kiss Bang Bang?

8 What was the name of the young central character in *The Omen*?

9 Who was the world's most famous Quasimodo?

10 What was the name of the 'destructive' and 'barbarous' figure played by Arnold Schwarzenegger?

11 Which movie character was employed as a nanny at 17 Cherry Tree Lane?

12 What was Rambo's first name?

13 Was Zorba the christian name or the surname of Zorba the Greek?

14 What does Eben and Sarah Kent's son become when he wants to?

15 In which 1962 movie did Omar Sharif play a character called Sherif Ali?

16 Which film character was built from 4000 pounds of Argentinian horse tails?

17 Which character in *The Wizard of Oz* held a chopper in his hand?

18 What was the name of the character played by this actress in this movie?

19 Who was Luke Skywalker's father?

20 Which starring character of a 1959 epic held the reins of Aldebaran, Altair, Antaros and Rigel?

1 Which movie featured Jodie Foster playing the part of a teenage hooker?

2 Which movie showed an assassin using a melon for target practice?

3 Which 1982 movie included a two-minute funeral scene that used a record 300 000 extras?

4 Which Charlton Heston movie inspired Emperor Hirohito to race out to a cinema for the first time — a) *Hiroshima Mon Amour* b) *Midway* or c) *Ben Hur*?

5 In which movie did this pair of 'ladies' steal the limelight from Marilyn Monroe?

6 Which 1982 movie cast Dustin Hoffman in drag?

7 Which movie had Marlon Brando riding into Wrightsville and taking over Bleakers Cafe?

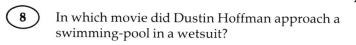

8 In which movie did Dustin Hoffman approach a swimming-pool in a wetsuit?

9 Which 1963 film had more than fifty stars in it?

10 Which movie featured Mel Brooks as a shrink at the Institute for the Very Very Nervous?

11 Of which movie was *The Wiz* a black version?

12 Which movie had gunslinger Frank Fuller arriving on the midday train?

13 Which 1980 movie, starring Jane Fonda, was about a nuclear accident?

14 Which 1966 movie was about Sir Thomas More's fall from favour with Henry VIII?

15 Which 1984 movie showed the consequences of Pol Pot's regime in Kampuchea?

16 In which movie did Susannah York and Beryl Reid play a lesbian couple?

17 Which movie opens with Billy Hayes being arrested for drug-smuggling at Istanbul airport?

18 What was the only movie on which production began *after* the death of the star?

19 Which 1986 Roman Polanski movie featured the most expensive single prop ever used?

20 Which Woody Allen movie contains a scene in which the hero walks out of the silver screen?

1 Who played Karen Silkwood in *Silkwood*?

2 Which movie is about a meeting in a hotel room between Marilyn Monroe and Albert Einstein?

3 Who was the subject of the first screen star biographical movie?

4 Which American president has been most portrayed on screen?

5 Which composer was the subject of the film *Song of Norway*?

6 Which film chronicled the adventures of the Hero of Aqaba, Liberator of Damascus and Uncrowned King of Arabia?

7 Which of these historical characters have appeared most regularly in movies —
a) Winston Churchill b) Cleopatra or c) Lenin?

8 Which historical character has been portrayed more times than any other — a) Shakespeare b) Abraham Lincoln or c) Napoleon?

9 Who played Al Jolson in *The Jolson Story*?

10 Which painter was portrayed by Kirk Douglas in *Lust for Life*?

11 Which movie star has been played on film by other actors more times than any other?

12 Which Anne was portrayed in *Anne of a Thousand Days*?

13 Who did Alec Guinnes play in the 1973 movie *The Last Ten Days*?

14 Which tragic film star was portrayed by Jessica Lange in the film *Frances*?

15 Who played this star in *Mommie Dearest*?

16 Who sang the voice-over for the songs in *The Jolson Story*?

17 Which leader was portrayed by Ingrid Bergman in *24 Hours In the Life of a Woman*?

18 Who played Hans Christian Andersen in the 1952 movie?

19 Who was the subject of the 1976 film *Goodbye Norma Jean*?

20 Who played Rudolph Valentino in the 1977 movie *Valentino*?

1 What is the first thing Clark Kent takes off before turning into this movie character?

2 Which 1982 movie starred 9-year-old Aileen Quinn?

3 Which children's movie was the top money-making film of the 1970s?

4 Who played Dr Dolittle?

5 Which child movie star became the US Ambassador to Ghana?

6 Which 1976 musical had an all-child cast?

7 On which fictional detective's adventures is the cartoon *Basil the Great Mouse Detective* based?

8 Which children's film starred Sally Ann Howes as Truly Scrumptious?

9 What did Dumbo hold in his trunk to enable him to fly?

10 Which family film starred a lioness called Elsa?

11 Which 1963 film was about a group of English schoolboys who turn to savagery when abandoned on a desert island?

12 Which movie originated the word 'supercalifragilisticexpialidocious'?

13 Which aquatic avian of cartoon fame was honoured on a San Marino postage stamp?

14 Who played Santa's chief elf in *Santa Claus the Movie*?

15 Who, as a child, starred in the 1960 movie *Pollyanna*?

16 In which country was *The Muppet Movie* censored because of gratuitous violence to Fozzie Bear?

17 What, according to a 1984 movie, should you never get wet or feed after midnight?

18 Which children's fairytale has been filmed more times than any other?

19 Where did the the Wizard of Oz live?

20 Which 1984 blockbuster, with a youthful following, was denounced for its 215 acts of violence including 14 killings and 39 attempted killings by the hero?

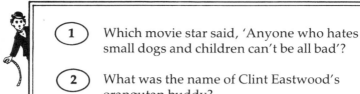

1 Which movie star said, 'Anyone who hates small dogs and children can't be all bad'?

2 What was the name of Clint Eastwood's orangutan buddy?

3 Who won an Oscar at the age of nine for her performance in *Paper Moon*?

4 Which child star said, 'I stopped believing in Santa Claus when I was six. Mother took me to see him in a department store and he asked me for my autograph'?

5 Which English actress started as a railway child before going *Walkabout*?

6 Which animal star had a personal valet, chef, limousine and chauffeur as well as a private suite at the film studio?

7 What craft did Shirley Temple sing about in the 1934 film *Bright Eyes*?

8 Who received her first screen kiss at the age of 14 in *The Blue Lagoon*?

9 Which animal star died in the arms of Jean Harlow — a) Rin Tin Tin   b) Lassie or c) Black Beauty?

10 Who was the star of *The Kid*?

11 With what kind of animal did Ronald Reagan star in *Bedtime for Bonzo*?

12 Which 1968 movie musical starred Mark Lester and Jack Wild?

13 Which disaster movie, starring Michael Caine and Olivia De Havilland, also included the largest cast of living creatures on film?

14 Which male child star grew up to be five feet three inches tall?

15 According to legend, which star was discovered at the age of 15 at Schwab's Drug Store?

16 Which 1973 movie about birds lists no credited human performers?

17 What is this animal and in which film did it appear?

18 In which 1944 movie did Elizabeth Taylor and Mickey Rooney play children who train a racehorse?

19 In which 1982 movie did seven-year-old Drew Barrymore play a leading role?

20 Which animal was voted the most popular movie performer of 1926?

1 What was this star's job in the movie *Brubaker*?

2 Who starred as stripper Gypsy Rose Lee in the 1962 movie *Gypsy*?

3 What was the profession of the hero of *The Citadel*?

4 What was Walter Matthau's occupation in *Cactus Flower*?

5 What was Jenny Agutter's profession in *An American Werewolf in London*?

6 Which movie was about the lives of entertainers Gertrude Lawrence and Noel Coward?

7 In which movie does Jack Lemmon play a clerk who advances his career by letting out his home to his bosses for illicit affairs?

8 What was Alan Bates's job in *Butley*?

9 In which film did Jeremy Irons play a Victorian fossil hunter?

10 In what kind of shop was Rocky's wife working when he first met her?

11 What is Richard Burton's profession in *Who's Afraid of Virginia Woolf*?

12 Which industry features in *How Green Was My Valley*?

13 What was Al Pacino's occupation in *Serpico*?

14 What was Jane Fonda's job in *9 to 5*?

15 What was Roy Scheider's position in the Jaws movies?

16 How did *The Sunshine Boys* make their living?

17 What was Diane Keaton's occupation in *Looking for Mr Goodbar*?

18 What was Greta Garbo's occupation in *Anna Christie*?

19 In which movie did Margaret Lockwood play a lady who turns to highway robbery?

20 What was David Niven's occupation in *Rough Cut* — a) safe-blower b) diamond polisher or c) policeman?

1. Which Steven Spielberg movie featured the Huey Lewis hit 'The Power Of Love'?

2. Which movie musical introduced the song 'Get Me To The Church On Time'?

3. Who sang 'The First Time' in *Play Misty For Me*?

4. Who sang 'As Time Goes By' in *Casablanca*?

5. Which songwriter complained about trying to find a rhyme for 'ghostbusters'?

6. Which movie musical introduced the song 'Maria'?

7. What world best-selling song came from the film *Holiday Inn*?

8. What is the most widely mimicked Al Jolson song?

9. Who wrote and performed the music for *Pat Garrett and Billy the Kid*?

10. Which musical featured the song 'Edelweiss'?

11. Which 1968 movie featured the songs 'Consider Yourself' and 'Food, Glorious Food'?

12. Which movie provided the hit song 'Summer Nights'?

13. Which Clint Eastwood film spawned a hit for Hugo Montenegro in 1968?

14. For which movie was Stevie Wonder's hit 'I Just Called To Say I love You' written?

15. Who wrote the hit theme song for *9 to 5*?

16 In which movie did this star sing 'Secret Love'?

17 Which movie's songs included 'Sweet Transvestite' and 'Science Fiction Double Feature'?

18 Which 1975 movie featured the Oscar-winning song 'I'm Easy'?

19 What was the Oscar-winning song in *Doctor Dolittle?*

20 For which movie did Deborah Harry and Giorgio Moroder write 'Call Me'?

1 Who has partnered Jill Ireland in 14 movies to date?

2 Which of these famous co-stars was born first — Doris Day or Rock Hudson?

3 Which famous couple co-starred in the 1969 movie *Boom*?

4 How many movies did Ginger Rogers and Fred Astaire co-star in — a) 9 b) 10 or c) 11?

5 Which two Johns played the leading roles in *Grease*?

6 Who is shown here, co-starring with Ann Sheridan in *I Was a Male War Bride*?

7 Who was Olivia De Havilland's most regular co-star?

8 Which actor did Laurence Olivier specifically request as his co-star in *Sleuth*?

9 Which 1968 box office success brought together the talents of Dustin Hoffman and Jon Voight?

10 Which two male stars shared top billing in the 'road' movies?

11 Who was Robert Redford's female co-star in *Legal Eagles*?

12 With whom did Glenn Ford star in *Gilda*?

13 Who was the female co-star in *Rebel Without a Cause*?

14 Who starred with Mae West in *My Little Chickadee*?

15 Which 1980 movie co-starred Laurence Olivier and Neil Diamond?

16 What was the second movie to team Robert Redford and Paul Newman?

17 With whom did Spencer Tracy co-star in ten movies?

18 Who went along with Charles Bronson and James Coburn from *The Magnificent Seven* to *The Great Escape*?

19 Who did Paulette Goddard star alongside in *Modern Times* and *The Great Dictator*?

20 Who co-starred with Jeanette MacDonald in eight movies?

1 To whom is Joanne Woodward married?

2 Which English couple were the first husband and wife team to win an Oscar each?

3 Who was Lauren Bacall's second husband?

4 Which actress is married to playwright Sam Shepard?

5 Which star of the movie *M*A*S*H* was married to Barbra Streisand?

6 Which star married Mickey Rooney, Artie Shaw and Frank Sinatra?

7 Was Rita Hayworth married to Orson Welles?

8 Which much-married star said, 'I'm the only man who has a marriage licence made out To Whom It May Concern'?

9 Which movie star was married to Carole Lombard from 1939 to 1942?

10 Which of his co-stars did Clint Eastwood marry?

11 Which actress declared, 'I'm a wonderful housekeeper. Every time I get divorced I keep the house'?

12 Which two beautiful blondes were married to John Derek before Bo?

13 Which actor married millionairess Barbara Hutton in 1942, thereby inspiring the joint nickname of 'Cash and Cary'?

14 Which film star's widow married and divorced David Frost?

15 How many years was James Cagney married to his wife Frances — a) 43 b) 53 or c) 63?

16 Which actress and long-time girlfriend of Randolph Hearst was guaranteed a daily mention in his newspapers?

17 Who has been married the most times — Elizabeth Taylor or Zsa Zsa Gabor?

18 To whom was Jean Peters married for 14 years, during which time no photo of them together was ever published?

19 Who was Greta Garbo's husband?

20 Who was this star's first husband?

(1) Who played this character's boss?

(2) Which movie introduced the spy Harry Palmer to the screen?

(3) Which detective was treated by Professor Freud in *The Seven Per Cent Solution*?

(4) Who played Joel Cairo in *The Maltese Falcon*?

(5) Which 'spy' movie introduced James Bond to a seven-foot-tall adversary with steel teeth?

(6) Which writer created Sam Spade?

(7) Which movie featured Jack Nicholson as a Californian private eye?

8 Which star was nominated for an Oscar for his performance in *The Spy Who Came In From The Cold*?

9 Who was the star of *The Ipcress File*?

10 What was the first name of the private eye called Shaft?

11 Which 1942 movie had Jack Benny and Carole Lombard as actors impersonating Nazis?

12 Who played Flint in *Our Man Flint*?

13 Which 1966 thriller starred Paul Newman as a double agent who goes to East Germany and is followed by his wife?

14 Who starred as Mata Hari in the 1932 movie of that name?

15 In which film did Virginia McKenna star as British spy Violette Szabo?

16 In which film musical did police officer Krupke appear?

17 Who starred as Inspector Clouseau in the 1968 film *Inspector Clouseau*?

18 Which private eye was played by Richard Rowntree?

19 Who was the female star of the 1984 spy thriller *The Little Drummer Girl*?

20 Which 1976 movie was about the two newspaper reporters who exposed the Watergate affair?

1 Which movie marked Robert Redford's debut as a director?

2 Who wrote and directed *Close Encounters of the Third Kind*?

3 Which British film director was awarded the American Film Institute's Life Achievement Award in 1978?

4 Who starred in and won an Oscar for directing the 1981 movie *Reds*?

5 Which actor directed the film *A Bridge Too Far*?

6 Which American artist subjected his audience to an eight-hour-long film about a man sleeping?

7 Who directed *A Passage to India*?

8 Which Russian director made *The Battleship Potemkin*?

9 Which British director has made controversial movies about composers Liszt, Mahler and Tchaikovsky?

10 Who wrote the screenplay of *The Misfits* specifically for Marilyn Monroe?

11 Who won a special Oscar for directing, producing and starring in the 1944 film *Henry V*?

12 Which 1983 movie did Barbra Streisand direct, produce, co-write and star in?

13 Who directed *Nashville*?

14 Who is the biggest money-making movie director of all time?

15 Who conceived, wrote and directed *The Producers*?

16 Which director made the first of his 34 brief screen appearances in *The Lodger*?

17 What was the first movie directed by this man?

18 Who directed the 1982 film *Fanny and Alexander*?

19 Who directed and starred in *Woman in Red*?

20 Who wrote and directed the 1916 film *Easy Street*?

THE ANSWERS

1 · TT · BIRDS AND BEASTS

1. Cheta — the picture shows Lex Barker as Tarzan
2. *Living Free*
3. *The Birds*
4. It was electrocuted
5. A diamond
6. An otter
7. A dog
8. Horse
9. Octopus — *Dear Octopus*
10. *Barbarella*
11. An otter
12. Long John Silver — each had a parrot
13. Bugs Bunny
14. Killer bees in *The Swarm*
15. *Jonathan Livingston Seagull*
16. Tweety Pie
17. An elephant
18. Edgar Allen Poe
19. Champion
20. *Cat on a Hot Tin Roof*

2 · MW · SETTINGS

1. The Rhine
2. Marseilles
3. Chicago
4. Berlin
5. Georgia
6. Ireland
7. New York
8. *Straw Dogs*
9. Bolivia
10. Hong Kong
11. *Deliverance*
12. Paris
13. Paris
14. Amity
15. Paris
16. *The Mission*
17. Texas
18. *Brief Encounter*
19. Death Valley — the picture shows a still from *Zabriskie Point*
20. Florence

3 · SR · WHO STARRED…?

1. Gene Hackman
2. Clark Gable
3. *The Towering Inferno*
4. Tom Cruise
5. *Gentlemen Prefer Blondes* — the picture shows Jane Russell and Marilyn Monroe
6. Jayne Mansfield
7. Mia Farrow
8. Anne Bancroft
9. David Niven
10. Tom Hulce
11. Sidney Poitier
12. Michael Caine
13. Christopher Lambert
14. Robert Shaw
15. Whoopi Goldberg
16. Nastassia Kinski
17. Errol Flynn
18. Olivia Hussey
19. James Caan
20. Mickey Rourke

4 · LT · ONLY IN HOLLYWOOD

1. *Krakatoa West of Java*
2. Joan Crawford
3. *Gone with the Wind*
4. Al Jolson
5. Wigs
6. Rex Harrison
7. Robert Redford
8. Shirley Temple
9. Rudolph Valentino
10. Joan Crawford
11. Howard Hughes
12. *Oklahoma!*
13. *Legal Eagles*
14. They were all midgets
15. *Heaven's Gate*
16. *Young Frankenstein*
17. Because he had a regular engagement to play clarinet in a jazz band, and he wouldn't break it — the picture shows Woody Allen
18. Walt Disney
19. Six
20. Raquel Welch

5 · SS · SCI-FI AND FANTASY

1. Jupiter
2. *Alien*
3. Thirty
4. *A Clockwork Orange*
5. Ming the Merciless and Flash Gordon
6. A De Lorean
7. Venus
8. *The Return of the Jedi*
9. David Bowie
10. *2010*
11. Krypton
12. John Hurt's
13. *Sleeper*
14. *Barbarella*
15. Harrison Ford
16. *2001: A Space Odyssey*
17. Blue
18. b) Mr Spock
19. *Invasion of the Body Snatchers*
20. Earth

6 MM · EARLY DAYS

1. Lillian Gish
2. Tom Mix
3. *Modern Times*
4. a) Australia
5. True
6. The Keystone Kops
7. Clara Bow
8. Buster Keaton
9. Charlie Chaplin
10. c) Fatty Arbuckle
11. Custard pies
12. His feet
13. Harold Lloyd
14. Hollywoodland
15. Rudolph Valentino
16. Theda Bara
17. Buster Keaton
18. Stan Laurel
19. Harold Lloyd
20. The left — the picture shows Charlie Chaplin

7 · TT · GOD SPOT

1. *Oh God!* — the picture shows George Burns
2. Yes
3. *Jesus Christ Superstar*
4. Cecil B. de Mille
5. *Quo Vadis*
6. Jennifer Jones
7. *Barbarella*
8. Warren Beatty
9. God
10. Harry Belafonte
11. *The Agony and the Ecstasy*
12. *It's a Wonderful Life*
13. Audrey Hepburn
14. *The Shoes of the Fisherman*
15. John Wayne
16. Peter Sellers
17. Richard Burton
18. Richard Burton
19. *The Singing Nun*
20. *The Greatest Story Ever Told*

8 · MW · DISNEY TIME

1. *Snow White and the Seven Dwarfs*
2. Donald Duck
3. *Peter Pan*
4. *The Living Desert*
5. Pinocchio
6. *Lady and the Tramp*
7. Mortimer
8. Donald Duck
9. A moustache
10. *Pinocchio*
11. *Treasure Island*
12. Herbie
13. Dopey
14. She was shot by a hunter
15. *Fantasia*
16. *Cinderella*
17. Mary Poppins
18. Daisy Duck
19. *The Sword in the Stone*
20. Tinkerbell's, in *Peter Pan* — the picture shows Marilyn Monroe

9 · SR · FIRSTS AND LASTS

1. Mickey Mouse
2. *Dragnet*
3. *Yankee Doodle Dandy*
4. *The Misfits*
5. Humphrey Bogart
6. Custard pies
7. *The Shootist*
8. Grace Kelly
9. Hedy Lamarr
10. *The Jazz Singer*
11. Max Factor
12. a) Elizabeth Taylor
13. Sylvester Stallone
14. *1984*
15. A beret
16. *To Have and Have Not*
17. *East of Eden* — the picture shows James Dean
18. *Tom Horn*
19. Queen Victoria
20. c) *Carry On Sergeant*

10 · LT · MAKING A NAME

1. The Legs — the picture shows Betty Grable
2. John Wayne
3. Hall
4. Greta Garbo
5. Roscoe
6. Norma Jean Baker
7. Michael Caine — from *The Caine Mutiny*
8. Groucho Marx
9. Sylvester Stallone
10. Bing Crosby
11. Rock Hudson
12. Lon Chaney
13. Stewart Grainger
14. The Marx Brothers
15. Mary Pickford
16. a) Francis X. Bushman
17. Richard Burton
18. Woody Allen
19. Abbott and Costello
20. Cary Grant

11 · SS · COPS AND CRIME

1. *Serpico*
2. San Francisco
3. The Keystone Kops
4. David Soul
5. *Key Largo*
6. The Bronx
7. *The Godfather Part Two*
8. Burt Lancaster
9. Mafia
10. Charles Bronson
11. *Papillon*
12. Chief Inspector Dreyfus
13. Frank Sinatra
14. Philip Marlowe
15. Audrey
16. James Cagney
17. *Klute*
18. *Little Caesar*
19. Harrison Ford
20. Callahan — the picture shows Clint Eastwood playing Dirty Harry

12 · MM · MOVIE MOGULS

1. D. W. Griffith
2. *The Ten Commandments*
3. Warner Brothers
4. Howard Hughes
5. Twice
6. Louis B. Mayer
7. Princess Grace of Monaco
8. D. W. Griffith
9. Samuel Goldwyn and Louis B. Mayer
10. King Vidor
11. United Artists Corporation
12. b) Goldfish
13. c) David O. Selznick
14. Rank
15. Samuel Goldwyn
16. Darryl F. Zanuck
17. Alfred Hitchcock
18. Ealing
19. RKO
20. Cannon

13 · TT · WHERE IN THE WORLD?

1. *Casablanca*
2. *An American in Paris*
3. *New York, New York*
4. Bashful Bend
5. *Blue Hawaii*
6. Texas
7. Hollywood
8. London
9. *Nashville*
10. *The Thief of Baghdad*
11. *From Russia with Love*
12. Los Angeles
13. *The Guns of Navarone*
14. *Manhattan*
15. *A Passage to India*
16. *Lady from Shanghai*
17. *Khartoum*
18. Venice — the picture shows Dirk Bogarde
19. Venice
20. Nuremberg — *Judgement at Nuremberg*

14 · MW · WORLD CINEMA

1. Australia
2. Andrzej Wajda
3. Josef Von Sternberg
4. India
5. Italy
6. *Les Enfants du Paradis*
7. Sweden
8. Luis Bunuel
9. *The Marriage of Maria Braun*
10. Gerard Depardieu
11. Jean-Luc Godard
12. *The Boat*
13. Sergei Eisenstein
14. Franco Zeffirelli
15. Jacques Tati
16. *Carmen*
17. Akira Kurosawa
18. Nastassia Kinski
19. c) Iceland
20. Werner Herzog

15 · SR · SUPPORTING CASTS

1. Bert Lahr
2. *Kramer vs Kramer*
3. Dorothy Lamour
4. *Citizen Kane*
5. David Niven
6. Gene Hackman
7. *The Women*
8. Horace Horsecollar
9. Joel Grey
10. *Rebecca*
11. Talia Shire
12. *Gone with the Wind*
13. Gabby Hayes
14. Bert Kwouk
15. *Gone with the Wind*
16. *Superman* — the picture shows Marlon Brando
17. E. T.
18. *Arsenic and Old Lace*
19. Lee Van Cleef
20. Maud Adams

16 · LT · THE END

1. James Cagney — the picture shows Humphrey Bogart
2. *Superman*
3. W. C. Fields
4. Gary Gilmore
5. James Cagney
6. Marilyn Monroe
7. *Giant*
8. Bing Crosby
9. James Dean
10. John Belushi
11. David Niven
12. Peter Finch
13. Charles Manson's
14. A cut-throat razor
15. Princess Grace of Monaco
16. Joe di Maggio
17. Charlie Chaplin
18. Rudolph Valentino
19. King Kong
20. A bra

17 · SS · HORROR MOVIES

1. Rosemary — in *Rosemary's Baby*
2. Vincent Price
3. Igor
4. Yes
5. Bob Hope
6. Bela Lugosi
7. *Friday the 13th*
8. The Hammer Studios
9. Count Dracula
10. *The Omen*
11. George Hamilton
12. Mike Oldfield
13. Sleeping
14. Green
15. Frankenstein's monster
16. *Carrie*
17. Bela Lugosi
18. *The Pit and the Pendulum*
19. Chocolate sauce
20. Freddy

18 · MM· OFF CAMERA

1. George Cukor
2. Howard Hughes
3. False eyelashes
4. Because the necklines of the costumes were too low. The film was *The Wicked Lady* starring Margaret Lockwood and James Mason
5. The MGM lion
6. Fatty Arbuckle
7. *One Million Years BC*
8. Facelifts
9. *The Elephant Man*
10. Scarlett O'Hara
11. Charlie Chaplin
12. *Earthquake*
13. Thomas Edison
14. The real thing
15. Chocolate
16. *Moby Dick*
17. *Alfie*
18. Marilyn Monroe
19. Liquorice
20. *Cleopatra*

19 · TT · NAMES

1. Dr Phibes
2. Alice
3. Eve
4. *Alfie*
5. Mr Chips
6. *Sebastiane*
7. *Rebecca*
8. *Ned Kelly*
9. *Queen Christina*
10. *Lolita*
11. Flicka — from *My Friend Flicka*
12. Ted and Alice
13. *Tammy*
14. *Whatever Happened to Baby Jane?*
15. Morgan
16. George
17. *Jezebel*
18. *Carrie*
19. *Harvey*
20. *Myra Breckinridge* — the picture shows Mae West

20 · MW · SONG AND DANCE

1. c) $10 million — the picture shows Cyd Charisse
2. Carmen Miranda
3. Frank Sinatra
4. *Xanadu*
5. *Funny Girl*
6. *The Sound of Music*
7. *The Tales of Beatrix Potter*
8. *Flashdance*
9. Gene Kelly
10. *Oklahoma!*
11. George Raft
12. *Gentlemen Prefer Blondes*
13. *Saturday Night Fever*
14. Rita Heyworth
15. Milk
16. Irene Castle
17. Fred Astaire
18. *Top Hat*
19. *Fame*
20. *At Long Last Love*

21 · SR · LEADING MEN

1. Mel Gibson
2. Laurence Olivier
3. Clark Gable
4. Roger Moore
5. Jack Lemmon
6. Italy
7. Dirk Bogarde
8. Anthony Quinn and Anthony Quayle
9. c) $4 million
10. George Burns
11. Clint Eastwood
12. Omar Sharif
13. Tom Conti
14. Arnold Schwarzenegger
15. Robert de Niro — the picture shows Meryl Streep
16. Lee Marvin
17. Humphrey Bogart
18. Martin Sheen
19. Clark Gable
20. Burt Reynolds

22 · LT · RELATIVELY SPEAKING

1. a) Chico
2. Geraldine Chaplin
3. Ernest Hemingway
4. Tony Curtis
5. b) Ginger Rogers
6. Princess Diana — the picture shows Errol Flynn
7. Sophia Loren
8. The Kennedys
9. Ryan and Tatum O'Neal
10. Shirley MacLaine
11. Donald Duck
12. b) Frenchie
13. Walter and John Huston
14. Great-great-great-grandson
15. Lynn and Vanessa Redgrave
16. Larry Hagman
17. Helena Bonham-Carter
18. Henry and Jane Fonda
19. Carrie Fisher
20. Judy Garland

23 · SS · MURDER, MYSTERY AND SUSPENSE

1. *Dressed to Kill*
2. *Play Misty For Me*
3. *Torn Curtain*
4. *Murder on the Orient Express*
5. She drowned
6. Edward Fox
7. *The Lady Vanishes*
8. She wrote it — she is crime writer Agatha Christie
9. *Airport*
10. *The Thin Man*
11. *The Thirty-Nine Steps*
12. *The Odessa File*
13. *Dial M For Murder* — the picture shows Grace Kelly
14. Sam Spade
15. Jack Nicholson
16. Vienna
17. Dorothy McGuire
18. *The Shining*
19. Charlotte Rampling
20. *Spellbound*

24 · MM · THEME SONGS

1. *Watership Down*
2. John Williams
3. *Gone with the Wind*
4. *The Sting*
5. Barry Gibb — the still is from *Grease*
6. Vangelis
7. 'Moon River'
8. Kenny Loggins
9. *Arthur*
10. *Deliverance*
11. Phil Collins
12. The Psychedelic Furs
13. John Williams
14. *The Mission*
15. Matt Monro
16. *A Star Is Born*
17. *You Only Live Twice*
18. David Bowie
19. *Saturday Night Fever*
20. *Rocky III*

25 · TT · TRANSPORT

1. On a motorcycle
2. 'The Chattanooga Choo Choo'
3. The sinking of the *Titanic*
4. Amy Johnson
5. A balloon
6. A train
7. *A Night at the Opera*
8. Cary Grant
9. *A Hard Day's Night*
10. Steve McQueen
11. A Ford Mustang
12. The Mississippi
13. The Atcheson, Topeka and the Santa Fe
14. Marianne Faithfull
15. An Aston Martin
16. *Easy Rider*
17. A train
18. A Triumph
19. A Model T
20. A Volkswagen — the picture shows Diane Keaton as Annie Hall

26 · MW · MY NAME IS BOND, JAMES BOND

1. *Doctor No* — the picture shows Ursula Andress
2. c) *Thunderball*
3. Jaws
4. George Lazenby
5. David Niven
6. Shirley Bassey
7. *Live and Let Die*
8. *Doctor No*
9. Shaken, not stirred
10. Fort Knox
11. *Live and Let Die*
12. Doctor No
13. SMERSH
14. *Casino Royale*
15. M
16. Honor Blackman
17. Miss Moneypenny
18. *Never Say Never Again*
19. Timothy Dalton
20. Oddjob

27 · SR · WHO PLAYED…?

1. Dame Peggy Ashcroft
2. Clint Eastwood
3. Warren Beatty
4. Alec Guinness
5. Jack Nicholson
6. Humphrey Bogart
7. Johnny Weissmuller
8. Liza Minnelli
9. Gary Cooper
10. Clint Eastwood
11. Ingrid Bergman
12. Michael J. Fox
13. Natalie Wood
14. Madonna
15. Dudley Moore
16. Dustin Hoffman
17. Ben Kingsley, star of *Gandhi*
18. David Hemmings
19. James Garner
20. Groucho Marx

28 · LT · NO EXPERIENCE REQUIRED

1. *The Killing Fields*
2. *Lady Sings the Blues*
3. Jacqueline Onassis
4. *Mad Max III* — the picture shows Tina Turner
5. Senator John Warner
6. Prince Sihanouk
7. Michael Jackson
8. Athol Fugard
9. Art Garfunkel of Simon and Garfunkel
10. Her brother, Viscount Althorp
11. Gough Whitlam
12. Dolly Parton
13. Hugh Hefner
14. Prince
15. Ernest Hemingway
16. Bob Geldof
17. Mick Jagger
18. Pat Nixon
19. Mikhail Baryshnikov
20. Darth Vader

29 · SS · OH WHAT A LOVELY WAR

1. *Where Eagles Dare*
2. Jack Hawkins
3. *The Dam Busters*
4. Anthony Quinn
5. The American Civil War
6. *The Eagle Has Landed*
7. John Wayne
8. *The Great Escape*
9. *Zulu*
10. *Coming Home*
11. World War I
12. Stormtroopers
13. Donald Sutherland
14. Russian roulette
15. A flying medal
16. Marlon Brando
17. The American Civil War
18. France
19. Korea
20. Major — the picture shows Loretta Swit in *M*A*S*H*

30 · MM · CINEMAS AND AUDIENCES

1. *The Blue Angel* — the picture shows Marlene Dietrich
2. *Chariots of Fire*
3. Saudi Arabia
4. a) the Cabbage
5. Joseph Stalin
6. Mickey Mouse
7. True
8. Paris
9. Three
10. The Lumiere Brothers
11. Dodge City
12. Jimmy Carter
13. c) TWA
14. The Trans-Siberian Railway
15. James Bond
16. a) Iran
17. Rin Tin Tin
18. c) The Roxy
19. a) Chile
20. Grauman's Chinese Theater

31 · TT · IN COLOUR

1. *Reflections in a Golden Eye*
2. Blue
3. White
4. Red
5. *Yellow Submarine*
6. *A Clockwork Orange*
7. Purple
8. *Bad Day at Black Rock*
9. *The Color Purple*
10. *Limelight*
11. The Scarlet Pimpernel
12. The Bluebird
13. Pink
14. The bride
15. *GI Blues* and *Blue Hawaii* — the picture shows Elvis Presley
16. *If…*
17. Yellow
18. Red
19. *Blacula*
20. *The Wizard of Oz*

32 · MW · STORYLINES

1. *Animal Crackers*
2. *Bugsy Malone*
3. *Three Days of the Condor*
4. *The Invisible Man*
5. She was a nun — the picture shows Julie Andrews
6. *The Third Man*
7. *The Dirty Dozen*
8. *Casablanca*
9. *Close Encounters of the Third Kind*
10. *Dog Day Afternoon*
11. *Sunday Bloody Sunday*
12. *Around the World in Eighty Days*
13. *The Servant*
14. *Marathon Man*
15. *The Go-Between*
16. *The Prime of Miss Jean Brodie*
17. *The French Connection*
18. *Chitty Chitty Bang Bang*
19. *Cool Hand Luke*
20. *Where Eagles Dare*

33 · SR · LEADING LADIES

1. Karen Blixen
2. Kim Basinger
3. Goldie Hawn
4. Mia Farrow
5. Sigourney Weaver
6. Ava Gardner
7. Ingrid Bergman
8. Greta Garbo
9. Sophia Loren
10. Julie Christie
11. Gina Lollobrigida
12. Brigitte Bardot
13. Elizabeth Taylor
14. Mel Brooks
15. Scarlett O'Hara, played by Vivien Leigh
16. Julie Andrews
17. Grace Kelly, Princess Grace of Monaco
18. Theda Bara
19. Doris Day
20. Shirley Temple

34 · LT · HOLLYWOOD LIVES

1. Groucho Marx
2. Sophia Loren
3. 60
4. Michelle Triola Marvin
5. Errol Flynn
6. Stacey Keach
7. Roberto Rossellini — the picture shows Ingrid Bergman
8. Paul Newman
9. Louise Brooks
10. Natalie Wood
11. Mae West
12. Clara Bow
13. *To Catch A Thief*
14. Elizabeth Taylor's breasts
15. Pickfair
16. Marilyn Monroe
17. Charlie Chaplin
18. Ali McGraw
19. Zsa Zsa Gabor
20. Marilyn Monroe's marriage to Arthur Miller

35 · SS · THE WILD WEST

1. *Blazing Saddles*
2. Robert Vaughan
3. *For A Few Dollars More*
4. The Sundance Kid
5. *High Noon*
6. Britain
7. *The Seven Samurai*
8. John Wayne
9. Trigger
10. Spaghetti westerns
11. *Butch Cassidy and the Sundance Kid*
12. Joan Crawford
13. *Destry Rides Again*
14. Annie Oakley
15. Roy Rogers
16. *Little Big Man*
17. *Destry Rides Again*
18. Buffalo Bill
19. *A Man Called Horse*
20. *True Grit* — the picture shows John Wayne

36 · MM · THE FILM OF THE BOOK

1. C. S. Forester — the still shows *The African Queen*
2. *Murder On the Orient Express*
3. *The Exorcist*
4. c) William Shakespeare
5. *Rebecca*
6. *2001: A Space Odyssey*
7. *Looking for Mr Goodbar*
8. *One Flew Over the Cuckoo's Nest*
9. *The Shining*
10. *Julia*
11. *Ben Hur*
12. Alexandre Dumas
13. Sherlock Holmes
14. Mary Shelley
15. Erich Segal
16. Raymond Chandler
17. Rudyard Kipling
18. *Jaws* and *Jaws II*
19. *The Poseidon Adventure*
20. Jules Verne

37 · TT · NUMBERS

1. Four — *The Four Just Men*
2. 10 — *10*
3. Deanna Durbin
4. One — *One of Our Dinosaurs is Missing*
5. One — *One from the Heart*
6. Sonja Henie
7. Three — *Three Coins in the Fountain*
8. Fourteen — *Seven Brides for Seven Brothers*
9. *Forty-Second Street*
10. Three — *The Three Faces of Eve*
11. Four — *The Four Feathers*
12. Twenty thousand — *Twenty Thousand Years in Sing Sing*
13. Dylan Thomas
14. Six — *Six Bridges to Cross*
15. Two — *Two Mules for Sister Sara*
16. Seven — *The Seven Year Itch*
17. *1984*
18. 39 — the still shows *The Thirty-Nine Steps*
19. *8½*
20. Ten — *Ten Little Indians*

38 · MW · X-RATED

1. Brooke Shields
2. Pinocchio
3. c) 73 inches
4. Marlon Brando — the picture shows Maria Schneider
5. b) The Bible Belt of North and South Carolina
6. *Emmanuelle*
7. Bob Guccione
8. Kissing — between Indian performers
9. *Deep Throat*
10. *Women in Love*
11. Angie Dickinson
12. *Limelight*
13. *Animal Farm*
14. No
15. Belgium
16. Parental Guidance
17. *Midnight Cowboy*
18. Fatty Arbuckle
19. The Hays Code
20. Adolf Hitler

39 · SR · QUOTE…UNQUOTE

1. *Love Story*
2. *On the Waterfront*
3. *The Sting*
4. *Gone with the Wind*
5. Clint Eastwood's
6. *Bonnie and Clyde*
7. *Psycho*
8. *Animal Crackers*
9. *Everything You Always Wanted to Know About Sex*
10. *Casablanca*
11. *Planet of the Apes*
12. *Rebecca*
13. Superman
14. *Mutiny On The Bounty*
15. *2001: A Space Odyssey*
16. *Seven Brides for Seven Brothers*
17. *A Streetcar Named Desire*
18. *The Maltese Falcon*
19. Mae West
20. 'Me Tarzan, you Jane' — the picture shows Johnny Weissmuller

40 · LT · PUT-DOWNS

1. Doris Day
2. *Cleopatra*
3. Barbra Streisand
4. Raquel Welch
5. Fred Astaire
6. Orson Welles
7. Tony Curtis
8. Joan Rivers — the picture shows Elizabeth Taylor
9. Jane Russell
10. Katharine Hepburn
11. Marilyn Monroe
12. Marlon Brando
13. Tallulah Bankhead
14. Marlon Brando
15. Bette Davis
16. Groucho Marx
17. Greta Garbo
18. Alfred Hitchcock
19. Elizabeth Taylor
20. Fred Astaire and Ginger Rogers

41 · SS · SPORT

1. The marathon — the picture shows Dustin Hoffman in *Marathon Man*
2. Pool
3. *Chariots of Fire*
4. Boxing
5. Boxing
6. *Players*
7. Robert de Niro
8. John Hurt
9. *Rollerball*
10. Ice hockey
11. *Rocky*
12. Vijay Amritraj
13. Muhammad Ali
14. Baseball
15. Groucho Marx
16. Sonja Henie
17. *Rocky*
18. Swimming
19. Soccer
20. Body building

42 · MM · THE OSCARS

1. *Out of Africa*
2. Lynn and Vanessa Redgrave
3. *All About Eve*
4. George Burns
5. Walt Disney
6. *On Golden Pond*
7. Katharine Hepburn
8. Woodstock
9. *True Grit*
10. Humphrey Bogart
11. Spencer Tracy
12. *The Godfather*
13. Shirley Temple
14. Sir John Gielgud
15. *The Godfather Part II*
16. Elizabeth Taylor
17. *The Kiss of the Spider Woman* — the picture shows William Hurt
18. Barbra Streisand
19. Yul Brynner
20. Gene Hackman

43 · TT · FASHION

1. Marlene Dietrich
2. A slipper — *The Slipper and the Rose*
3. Audrey Hepburn
4. *10*
5. Joan Crawford
6. *Mahogany* — the picture shows Diana Ross
7. Dorothy Lamour
8. Trousers
9. A deerstalker
10. Clark Gable
11. Nancy Kwan — in *The World of Suzie Wong*
12. Cecil Beaton
13. *The Wild One*
14. The cane
15. Shirley Temple
16. *Barbarella*
17. Yul Brynner
18. With their boots on
19. Madonna
20. Annie Hall

44 · MW · CHARACTERS

1. The Cisco Kid
2. Elliot
3. Scarlett O'Hara
4. *Dressed To Kill*
5. *Casablanca*
6. Sherlock Holmes
7. James Bond
8. Damien
9. Charles Laughton
10. Conan
11. Mary Poppins
12. John
13. The surname
14. Superman
15. *Lawrence of Arabia*
16. King Kong
17. The Tin Man
18. Sally Bowles — the picture shows Liza Minnelli in *Cabaret*
19. Darth Vader
20. Ben Hur

45 · SR · WHICH MOVIE?

1. *Taxi Driver*
2. *The Day of the Jackal*
3. *Gandhi*
4. c) *Ben Hur*
5. *Some Like It Hot* — the picture shows Tony Curtis and Jack Lemmon
6. *Tootsie*
7. *The Wild One*
8. *The Graduate*
9. *It's a Mad, Mad, Mad, Mad World*
10. *High Anxiety*
11. *The Wizard of Oz*
12. *High Noon*
13. *The China Syndrome*
14. *A Man for All Seasons*
15. *The Killing Fields*
16. *The Killing of Sister George*
17. *Midnight Express*
18. *The Trail of the Pink Panther*
19. *Pirates*
20. *The Purple Rose of Cairo*

46 · LT · REAL LIVES

1. Meryl Streep
2. *Insignificance*
3. Charlie Chaplin
4. Abraham Lincoln
5. Franz Liszt
6. *Lawrence of Arabia*
7. c) Lenin
8. c) Napoleon
9. Larry Parks
10. Vincent Van Gogh
11. Charlie Chaplin
12. Anne Boleyn
13. Adolf Hitler
14. Frances Farmer
15. Faye Dunaway — the picture shows Joan Crawford
16. Al Jolson
17. Golda Meir
18. Danny Kaye
19. Marilyn Monroe
20. Rudolf Nureyev

47 · SS · KID'S STUFF

1. His glasses — the picture shows Christopher Reeves as Superman
2. *Annie*
3. *Star Wars*
4. Rex Harrison
5. Shirley Temple
6. *Bugsy Malone*
7. Sherlock Holmes
8. *Chitty Chitty Bang Bang*
9. A feather
10. *Born Free*
11. *Lord of the Flies*
12. *Mary Poppins*
13. Donald Duck
14. Dudley Moore
15. Hayley Mills
16. New Zealand
17. A Gremlin
18. *Cinderella*
19. The Emerald City
20. *Indiana Jones and the Temple of Doom*

48 · MM · NEVER WORK WITH…

1. W. C. Fields
2. Clyde
3. Tatum O'Neal
4. Shirley Temple
5. Jenny Agutter
6. Rin Tin Tin
7. 'The Good Ship Lollipop'
8. Brooke Shields
9. a) Rin Tin Tin
10. Jackie Coogan
11. A chimpanzee
12. *Oliver!*
13. *The Swarm*
14. Mickey Rooney
15. Lana Turner
16. *Jonathan Livingston Seagull*
17. A pushmi-pullu — from the movie *Doctor Dolittle*
18. *National Velvet*
19. *E. T.*
20. Rin Tin Tin

49 · TT · WORKING LIVES

1. Prison governor — the picture shows Robert Redford
2. Natalie Wood
3. Medicine
4. Dentistry
5. Nursing
6. *Star!*
7. *The Apartment*
8. A college lecturer
9. *The French Lieutenant's Woman*
10. A pet shop
11. College professor
12. Coal mining
13. Policeman
14. Typist
15. Police chief
16. They were comedians
17. Teaching
18. A prostitute
19. *The Wicked Lady*
20. c) Policeman

50 · MW · SONGS FROM THE MOVIES

1. *Back to the Future*
2. *My Fair Lady*
3. Roberta Flack
4. Dooley Wilson
5. Ray Parker Jr
6. *West Side Story*
7. 'White Christmas'
8. 'Mammy'
9. Bob Dylan
10. *The Sound of Music*
11. *Oliver!*
12. *Grease*
13. *The Good, The Bad and the Ugly*
14. *The Woman in Red*
15. Dolly Parton
16. *Calamity Jane* — the picture shows Doris Day
17. *The Rocky Horror Picture Show*
18. *Nashville*
19. 'Talk To The Animals'
20. *American Gigolo*

51 · SR · CO-STARS

1. Charles Bronson
2. Doris Day
3. Richard Burton and Elizabeth Taylor
4. c) 11
5. John Travolta and Olivia Newton-John
6. Cary Grant
7. Errol Flynn
8. Michael Caine
9. *Midnight Cowboy*
10. Bob Hope and Bing Crosby
11. Deborah Winger
12. Rita Hayworth
13. Natalie Wood
14. W. C. Fields
15. *The Jazz Singer*
16. *The Sting*
17. Katharine Hepburn
18. Steve McQueen
19. Charlie Chaplin
20. Nelson Eddy

52 · LT · MARRIAGE LINES

1. Paul Newman
2. Laurence Olivier and Vivien Leigh
3. Jason Robards
4. Jessica Lange
5. Elliott Gould
6. Ava Gardner
7. Yes
8. Mickey Rooney
9. Clark Gable
10. Sondra Locke
11. Zsa Zsa Gabor
12. Ursula Andress and Linda Evans
13. Cary Grant
14. Peter Sellers' widow
15. c) 63
16. Marion Davies
17. Zsa Zsa Gabor
18. Howard Hughes
19. She did not marry
20. Humphrey Bogart — the picture shows Lauren Bacall

53 · SS · SPIES AND SLEUTHS
1. Herbert Lom — the picture shows Peter Sellers as Inspector Clouseau
2. *The Ipcress File*
3. Sherlock Holmes
4. Peter Lorre
5. *The Spy Who Loved Me*
6. Dashiell Hammett
7. *Chinatown*
8. Richard Burton
9. Michael Caine
10. John
11. *To Be or Not To Be*
12. James Coburn
13. *Torn Curtain*
14. Greta Garbo
15. *Carve Her Name with Pride*
16. *West Side Story*
17. Alan Arkin
18. Shaft
19. Diane Keaton
20. *All the President's Men*

54 · MM · WRITERS AND DIRECTORS
1. *Ordinary People*
2. Steven Spielberg
3. Alfred Hitchcock
4. Warren Beatty
5. Richard Attenborough
6. Andy Warhol
7. David Lean
8. Sergei Eisenstein
9. Ken Russell
10. Arthur Miller
11. Laurence Olivier
12. *Yentl*
13. Robert Altman
14. Steven Spielberg
15. Mel Brooks
16. Alfred Hitchcock
17. *Citizen Kane* — the picture shows Orson Welles
18. Ingmar Bergman
19. Gene Wilder
20. Charlie Chaplin

Photographic Acknowledgements
Photographs courtesy of The Kobal Collection

Picture research by Sheila Corr